The Book of Political & Business One-liners

The Book of Political & Business One-liners

Jenny Hunter

NEW HOLLAND

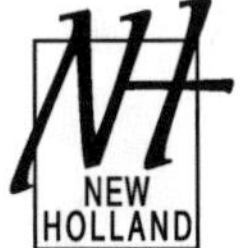

First published in Australia in 2008 by
New Holland Publishers (Australia) Pty Ltd
Sydney • Auckland • London • Cape Town

1/66 Gibbes Street Chatswood NSW 2067 Australia
218 Lake Road Northcote Auckland New Zealand
86 Edgware Road London W2 2EA United Kingdom
80 McKenzie Street Cape Town 8001 South Africa

National Library of Australia Cataloguing-in-Publication Data:

Hunter, Jenny, 1955-
Book of political and business one-liners / author, Jenny Hunter.

ISBN 9781741106176 (pbk.)

Political science--Quotations, maxims, etc.
Business--Quotations, maxims, etc.

320

Publisher: Martin Ford
Managing Editor: Lliane Clarke
Junior Editor: Sally Hills
Designer: Natasha Hayles
Production Assistant: Liz Malcolm
Printer: Publisher's Graphics, Carol Stream IL.

10 9 8 7 6 5 4 3 2 1

About the author

Jenny Hunter has researched and edited three previous books for New Holland—*True Blue Guide to Australian Slang, The Book of Great One-liners* and *The Aussie Fact Book*. Jenny also works in an assortment of roles including managing websites and assisting with the annual Garma Festival (a festival of Aboriginal culture). She lives in Manly (NSW) with her partner and teenage son.

Contents

Introduction

This book is a collection of one-liners and quotations from both the business and politics worlds.

Both involve many forthright high-profile figures, with a lot to say. Some of these figures are essentially 'multi-mediocre' personalities who nevertheless have occasionally uttered memorable lines. Others have displayed a consistently high level of verbal mastery, originality, accuracy and humour.

Politicians probably say more in public than any other profession, and while a small percentage of their verbiage is memorable, some, such as Churchill and Keating, are very quotable and are therefore prominent in this collection.

Management gurus, including management writer Peter Drucker, feature strongly as does legendary share market investor Warren Buffett, aka 'the Oracle of Omaha'.

Also included are one-liners, *bon-mots*, remarks, observations and 'perfect thoughts' from feminists, comedians, writers, scientists and philosophers plus some famous phrases which have become part of everyday language.

Former Australian prime minister Paul Keating once said 'I'm in the grenade throwing business. Occasionally I drop one beside my foot, but I get many direct hits.' Keating's verbal brilliance is complemented by his originality with ideas—a trait which he characterised when he said, 'Politics has always been an ideas market. When you run the ideas, you run the market.'

Most of us don't get the opportunity to use words as 'grenades', but that shouldn't stop us appreciating and occasionally borrowing from the 'grenade throwers'.

Ability and character

One should not be braver than one's ability.

Jack Brabham, Australian Formula One racing car champion

Your attitude, not your aptitude, will determine your altitude.

Zig Ziglar, American motivational writer and speaker

I was and remain, as a person and as a prime minister, an optimist. Politics may be the art of the possible but at least in life give the impossible a go.

Tony Blair, former British Labour prime minister

The human mind is like an umbrella—it functions best when open.

Walter Gropius (1883–1969), German-American architect

My main job was developing talent. I was a gardener providing water and other nourishment to our top 750 people. Of course, I had to pull out some weeds, too.

Jack Welch, American, former General Electric CEO

Arrogance is a killer, and wearing ambition on one's sleeve can have the same effect. There is a fine line between arrogance and self-confidence.

Jack Welch

Nothing gives a person so much advantage over another as to remain always cool and unruffled under all circumstances.

Thomas Jefferson (1743–1826), American president

If I had the choice of hiring someone with connections or someone with skills and talent, I'd go with the latter.

Chip Goodyear, American, BHP Billiton CEO

A man of character finds a special attractiveness in difficulty, since it is only by coming to grips with difficulty that he can realise his potentialities.

Charles de Gaulle (1890–1970), French president

I may lose many things including my temper, but I do not lose my nerve.

Jawaharlal Nehru (1889–1964), Indian prime minister

Never try to be an expert if you are not. Build on your strengths and find strong people to do the other necessary tasks.

Peter Drucker (1909–2005), American-Austrian management academic and writer

My information was that he had a plastic hose, a canary and a geranium and they made him Minister for Primary Industry.

Fred Daly (1913–1995), Australian Labor politician, about conservative minister Sir William McMahon

A professional is a person who can do his best at a time when he doesn't particularly feel like it.

Alistair Cooke (1908–2004), English-American writer

Whenever you are asked if you can do a job, tell 'em, 'Certainly, I can!' Then get busy and find out how to do it.

Theodore Roosevelt (1858–1919), American president

I am a Ford not a Lincoln.

Gerald Ford (1909–2006), American president and vice president. Using a play on words (or cars) in a speech as vice president on his skills as a public speaker compared to Abraham Lincoln. Lincoln's Gettysburg Address is frequently used as an example of exemplary speech-making.

Advertising, marketing and propaganda

I decided to use myself to promote my company.

Sir Richard Branson, British businessman and founder of the Virgin Group

If by turning up in a captain's outfit to promote our airline, it gave photographers a better picture, then I'd turn up in a captain's outfit. I'd feel kind of goofy sometimes, but if it got on the front pages of newspapers across the world ... that's £5 million of advertising.

Sir Richard Branson

The 30-second spot—at least as it exists today—is either dead, dying or has outlived its usefulness.

Joseph Jaffe, American-South African marketing and advertising commentator and author

I'd rather describe it as 'authentic marketing' because I think 'green marketing' sounds as though there's some sort of spin to it.

Sophie Bartho, Australian businesswoman

When the product is right, you don't have to be a great marketer.

Lee Iacocca, American business executive

Propaganda is to a democracy what the bludgeon is to a totalitarian state.

Noam Chomsky, Canadian philosopher

It is not necessary to advertise food to hungry people, fuel to cold people, or houses to the homeless.

John Kenneth Galbraith (1908–2006), American-Canadian economist

Strategy and timing are the Himalayas of marketing. Everything else is the Catskills.

Al Ries and Jack Trout, American advertising executives and co-authors of *The Battle for Your Mind.* The Catskill Mountains are in New York State with the highest elevation being 4180 feet whereas the highest mountain in the world (Everest) is part of the Himalayas.

Advertising may be described as the science of arresting the human intelligence long enough to get money from it.

Stephen Leacock (1869–1944), Canadian academic

The aim of marketing is to make selling superfluous.

Peter Drucker (1909–2005), American-Austrian management academic and writer

If you don't sell, it's not the product that's wrong, it's you.

Estee Lauder (1907–2004), American businesswoman

Like the movement to combat environmental pollution, the next consumer-led reaction will be against the mental pollution caused by marketers.

Faith Popcorn, American futurist, a 2007 prediction

Of course you sell candidates for political office the same way you sell soap or sealing wax or whatever; because, when you get right down to it, that's the only way anything is sold.

Sid Bernstein (1907–1993), American advertising guru known as 'Mr Advertising'

You can tell the ideals of a nation by its advertisements.

Norman Douglas (1868–1952), British writer

History will see advertising as one of the real evil things of our time. It is stimulating people constantly to want things, want this, want that.

Malcolm Muggeridge (1903–1990), British journalist

The philosophy behind much advertising is based on the old observation that every man is really two men—the man he is and the man he wants to be.

William Feather (1889–1981), American publisher and writer

I know half the money I spend on advertising is wasted, but I can never find out which half.

John Wanamaker (1838–1932), American businessman often called the 'father of advertising'

We've complacently agreed that culture is a synonym for entertainment. We've become consumers, not epicureans. We applaud people who market things rather than make things.

A.A. Gill, British newspaper columnist

Advice and inspiration

My greatest strength as a consultant is to be ignorant and ask a few questions.

Peter Drucker (1909–2005), American-Austrian management academic and writer

Anything is possible if you have the nerve.

J.K. Rowling, British author of the *Harry Potter* series of books

The greater the obstacle, the more glory in overcoming it.

Molière (1622–1673), French playwright and actor

It is not only for what we do that we are held responsible, but also for what we do not do.

Molière

You pay for my head, and I throw in my heart for free.

James Carville, American political consultant best known for his advice to Bill Clinton during his successful 1992 presidential campaign

I have walked that long road to freedom. I have tried not to falter; I have made missteps along the way. But I have discovered the secret that after climbing a great hill, one only finds that there are more hills to climb.

Nelson Mandela, former South African president

A good head and a good heart are always a formidable combination.

Nelson Mandela

It's the hope of slaves sitting around a fire singing freedom songs; the hope of immigrants setting out for distant shores; the hope of a young naval lieutenant bravely patrolling the Mekong Delta; the hope of a millworker's son who dares to defy the odds; the hope of a skinny kid with a funny name who believes that America has a place for him, too. The audacity of hope!

Barack Obama, American Democrat senator and 2008 presidential candidate

Too bad all the people who know how to run the country are busy driving taxi cabs and cutting hair.

George Burns (1896–1996), American comedian

We don't see things as they are, we see things as we are.

Anais Nin (1903–1977), French-American writer

It's more fun to be a pirate than to join the Navy.

Steve Jobs, American businessman and founder of Apple Computers in 1982 about his rebellious approach to business and management

The usefulness of an opinion is itself a matter of opinion.

John Stuart Mill (1806–1873), British economist and philosopher

No-one wants advice—only corroboration.

John Steinbeck (1902–1968), American Nobel-prize winning writer

Advisers advise and ministers decide.

Margaret Thatcher, former British prime minister

Good advice is something a man gives when he is too old to set a bad example.

François de La Rochefoucauld (1613–1680), French writer

Amnesia defence

The only honest answer is that try as I might, I cannot recall anything whatsoever ...

Ronald Reagan (1911–2004), American president. Late in his presidency (1981–89) Reagan was asked, at an official inquiry, about his recollection of the Iran-Contra scandal.

I don't recall.

Alan Bond, Australian businessman. In a 1994 federal Court fraud case, Bond was asked whether he had money in offshore trusts and Swiss bank accounts following the collapse of his company Bell Resources.

I do not have a specific recollection of having received or read this cable or of it otherwise being brought to my attention.

Alexander Downer, Australian Foreign Minister. The 2006 Oil for Food Inquiry investigated who knew what about the payment of AU$300 million to a Jordanian trucking company during the UN's Oil for Food program.

I can't recall thinking that at the time.

Mark Vaile, Australian Deputy Prime Minister, to the 2006 Oil for Food Inquiry

My recollection doesn't take me there.

Trevor Flugge, former Australian Wheat Board (AWB) chairman to the 2006 Oil for Food Inquiry

I can't recall. I honestly can't recall.

Andrew Lindberg, former Australian Wheat Board executive to the 2006 Oil for Food Inquiry

I don't recall the detail, Mr Urquhart, but I can speculate if you want.

Brian Burke, former Western Australian premier at the 2007 Western Australia Corruption and Crime Commission hearing into the former WA premier's attempts to influence current state government ministers

Beliefs and -isms

I am a fairly conservative white picket fence man as everyone knows.

John Howard, Australian Prime Minister

In future, welfare will be a hand-up not a handout.

Tony Blair, former British Labour prime minister

Let's not talk about communism. Communism was just an idea, just pie in the sky.

Boris Yeltsen (1931–2007), Russian president

Communism is like prohibition; it's a good idea but it won't work.

Will Rogers (1879–1935), American actor and writer

Puritanism: the haunting fear that someone, somewhere, may be happy.

H.L. Mencken (1880–1956), American journalist

A faith is something you die for; a doctrine is something you kill for: there is all the difference in the world.

Tony Benn, former British Labour minister who became increasingly left wing during his parliamentary career

The liberty of the individual must be thus far limited; he must not make himself a nuisance to other people.

John Stuart Mill (1806–1873), British economist and philosopher

I never meant to say that the Conservatives are generally stupid. I meant to say that stupid people are generally Conservative. I believe that is so obviously and universally admitted a principle that I hardly think any gentleman will deny it.

John Stuart Mill

One person with a belief is equal to a force of ninety-nine who have only interests.

John Stuart Mill

With some notable exceptions, businessmen favour free enterprise in general but are opposed to it when it comes to themselves.

Milton Friedman (1912–2006), American economist

You can't get good Chinese takeout in China and Cuban cigars are rationed in Cuba. That's all you need to know about communism.

P.J. O'Rourke, American writer

The Tory recognises the contrast between *laissez–faire* and *noblesse oblige*.

Michael Heseltine, former British Conservative minister

We know what happens to people who stay in the middle of the road. They get run down.

Aneurin Bevan (1897–1960), British Labour politician

Focusing your life solely on making a buck shows a certain poverty of ambition. It asks too little of yourself. Because it's only when you hitch your wagon to something larger than yourself that you realise your true potential.

Barack Obama, American Democrat senator and 2008 American presidential candidate

None of our institutions exists by itself and as an end in itself. Every one is an organ of society and exists for the sake of society. Business is no exception. 'Free enterprise' cannot be justified as being good for business. It can only be justified as being good for society.

Peter Drucker (1909–2005), American-Austrian management academic and writer

Those who stand for nothing fall for anything.

Alexander Hamilton (1755–1804), American politician

Hedonism may not be acknowledged as a traditional religion but it is nevertheless a belief system that in effect shapes the behaviour of the individual (known as consumers in the church of Australian business).

Bernard Salt, Australian demographer and writer

Pennies don't fall from heaven. They have to be earned on earth.

Margaret Thatcher, former British prime minister

Socialism failed because it couldn't tell the economic truth; capitalism may fail because it couldn't tell the ecological truth.

Lester Brown, American enviromentalist

A stand can be made against invasion by an army; no stand can be made against invasion by an idea.

Victor Hugo (1802–1885), French writer

The greatest dangers to liberty lurk in insidious encroachment by men of zeal, well meaning but without understanding.

Louis D. Brandeis (1856–1941), American jurist

If we believe a thing to be bad, and if we have a right to prevent it, it is our duty to try to prevent it and to damn the consequences.

Lord Milner (1854–1925), British colonial administrator

Democracy and socialism are a means to an end, not the end itself.

Jawaharlal Nehru (1889–1964), Indian prime minister

The difficulty lies, not in the new ideas, but in escaping from the old ones, which ramify, for those brought up as most of us have been, into every corner of our minds.

John Maynard Keynes (1883–1946), British economist

The term socialist has had its day ... it has been appropriated by the communist bloc. But let them have it, let's use some other term like equity or social justice.

Bob Carr, Australian former NSW Labor premier

Boom and bust

It's all about ego. Bondy wants to return to Perth dressed in a toga with $1 billion in his bank account. He wants to say, 'I'm Bond, I'm back, I've got a diamond mine in Africa, an oil well in Madagascar'.

Rob Still, South African entrepreneur and Alan Bond sceptic in 2007 about the return to the businessworld of the Australian convicted fraudster

I guess ego took over, they reckoned they could cut the legs off Telstra.

Bob Mansfield, Australian former Telstra chairman about the failed telecommunications company, One.Tel, which imploded in 2001 following questionable financial practices by the entrepreneurial management team

I've got balls of steel. Some investors have been great and have been very supportive. But some of these city people act like a bunch of cry babies.

Mike Ashley, reclusive British billionaire

We're the beneficiaries of a mining boom. It has been raining gold bars.

Wayne Swan, Australian federal Labor shadow treasurer

Although it's easy to forget sometimes, a share is not a lottery ticket ... it's part-ownership of a business.

Peter Lynch, American investor and financial advisor

Many investors seem to have forgotten a hard reality: There are frequent periods when stock markets don't do much.

Jim Rogers, American investor and co-founder with George Soros of the Quantum Fund

It's not whether you're right or wrong, but how much money you make when you're right and how much you lose when you're wrong. You attain superior long-term returns through preservation of capital and home runs. I'm not better than the next trader, just quicker at admitting my mistakes and moving on to the next opportunity.

George Soros, American-Hungarian investor and co-founder of the Quantum Group of Funds

> There weren't enough boring people in the company. There weren't enough men in brown cardigans.
>
> An Australian management consultant about One.Tel's entrepreneurial management team

Born to rule

The Cecils always end up on top.

Tony Benn, former British Labour minister

Not a reluctant peer but a persistent commoner.

Tony Benn, who was born in a family of peers but rejected this background by joining the Labour Party and becoming increasingly left wing

I am the 10th Prime Minister of Queen Elizabeth II's reign. So she has pretty much the measure of us by now.

Tony Blair, former British Labour prime minister at the Queen's golden wedding celebration in 1997

There can be no place in a 21st century parliament for people with 15th century titles upholding 19th century prejudices.

Paddy Ashdown, British Liberal Democrat politician

Gentility is what is left over from rich ancestors after the money is gone.

John Ciardi (1916–1986), American poet and translator

Members rise from CMG (known sometimes in Whitehall as 'Call Me God') to the KCMG ('Kindly Call Me God') to—for a select few governors and super-ambassadors—the GCMG ('God calls Me God').

Anthony Sampson (1926–2004), British journalist

If at any stage people feel that the Monarchy has no further part to play, then for goodness sake let's end the thing on amicable grounds without having a row.

Prince Philip, Queen Elizabeth II's husband about debate in some Commonwealth nations about becoming republics

It is about time we had an end to the old Britain, where all that matters is the privileges you were born with, rather than the potential you actually have.

Gordon Brown, British Labour prime minister

I shall be an autocrat: that's my trade. And the good Lord will forgive me: that's his.

Catherine the Great (1729–1796), Russian empress

She understands that more can be achieved by example than with rhetoric. That does not sit easily in an age of celebrity revelations.

William Shawcross, British writer, about Queen Elizabeth II of Great Britain and Northern Ireland

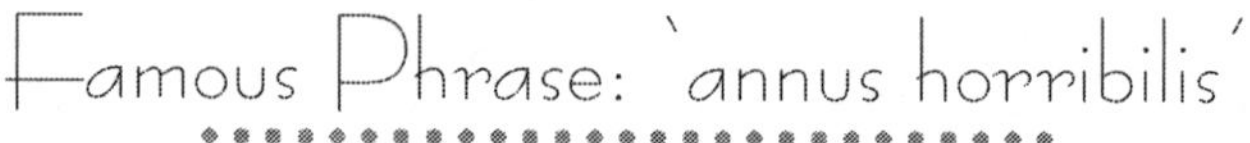

In the words of one of my more sympathetic correspondents, it has turned out to be an '*annus horribilis*'.

Queen Elizabeth II of Great Britain and Northern Ireland in 1992, the year three of her children (Charles, Andrew and Anne) separated from their spouses and Windsor Castle was damaged by fire

Business

I never get the accountants in before I start up a business. It's done on gut feeling, especially if I can see that they are taking the mickey out of the consumer.

Sir Richard Branson, British businessman and founder of the Virgin Group

So the question is, do corporate executives, provided they stay within the law, have responsibilities in their business activities other than to make as much money for their stockholders as possible? And my answer to that is, no they do not.

Milton Friedman (1912–2006), American economist

Running a company on market research is like driving while looking in the rear-view mirror.

Dame Anita Roddick (1942–2007), British businesswoman and founder of The Body Shop

A business that makes nothing but money is a poor kind of business.

Henry Ford (1863–1947), American, founder of the Ford Motor Company

Apple's market share is bigger than BMW's or Mercedes' or Porsche's in the automotive market. What's wrong with being BMW or Mercedes?

Steve Jobs, American businessman and founder of Apple Computers

You have to have your heart in the business and the business in your heart.

Thomas J. Watson (1874–1956), American businessman and IBM president

Big business is only small business with an extra nought on it.

Robert Holmes a Court (1937–1990), Australian businessman

My son is now an 'entrepreneur'. That's what you're called when you don't have a job.

Ted Turner, American businessman and founder of CNN

Monopoly is a terrible thing, till you have it.

Rupert Murdoch, Australian-American businessman

Market discipline is very aggressive, very strong and very precise in who it clobbers—those who don't perform. There's only one blemish in capitalism and that is when market discipline is lost to a monopolist.

Scott McNealy, American co-founder and former Sun Microsystems CEO

We did the sort of thing you probably shouldn't ever do: put a shingle up and give it a catchy name.

Edmund George, Australian businessman and co-founder of holySheet!

That's the problem with prosperity—it hides the defects of a business.

Harvey Firestone (1868–1938), American businessman

A good decision executed well often beats a brilliant one implemented poorly.

Dale Cottrell, Australian management consultant

I have no use for bodyguards, but I have very special use for two highly trained certified public accountants.

Elvis Presley (1935–1977), American entertainer

Change

The urgent question of our time is whether we can make change our friend and not our enemy.

Bill Clinton, American Democrat president in his 1993 inaugural speech

I was trying to shake up a culture of paralysis. Hiding behind data or precedents to avoid making a decision had to stop.

Stuart Rose, British, Marks & Spencer chief executive

Willingness to change is a strength, even if it means plunging part of the company into total confusion for a while.

Jack Welch, American, former General Electric CEO

Faced with the choice between changing one's mind and proving that there is no need to do so, almost everyone gets busy on the proof.

John Kenneth Galbraith (1908–2006), American-Canadian economist

Change is the law of life. And those who look only to the past or present are certain to miss the future.

John F. Kennedy (1917–1963), American president

Never doubt that a small group of thoughtful committed citizens can change the world. Indeed, it is the only thing that ever has.

Margaret Mead (1901–1978), American anthropologist

Change is one thing, progress is another. 'Change' is scientific, 'progress' is ethical; change is indubitable, whereas progress is a matter of controversy.

Bertrand Russell (1872–1970), British philosopher and mathematician

I didn't come into politics to change the Labour Party. I came into politics to change the country.

Tony Blair, former British Labour prime minister

Change can take place only when liberal and radical pressures are both strong ... Liberals never know whether the door is unlocked because they are afraid to try it. Radicals, on the other hand, miss many opportunities for small advances because they are unwilling to settle for so little.

Philip Slater, American sociologist

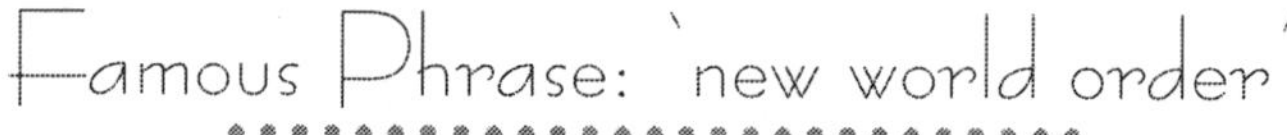

And now, we can see a new world coming into view. A world in which there is the very real prospect of a new world order.

George Bush Sr, former American president, in a speech after the end of the Cold War and before the 1991 Gulf War

Climate change and environment

We've announced a £200 million 'eco-plan'—we're calling it 'Plan A' (because we don't have a Plan B)—that will shape everything about the way we do business.

Stuart Rose, British, Marks & Spencer chief executive

There were record high temperatures yesterday. I blame Al Gore. Until he invented this global warming, none of this stuff happened.

Jimmy Kimmel, American comedian

Mankind has probably done more damage to the earth in the 20th century than in all of previous human history.

Jacques Cousteau (1910–1997), French adventurer

We're in a giant car heading towards a brick wall and everyone's arguing over where they're going to sit.

David Suzuki, Canadian scientist and environmental activist

This concentration of [media] power helps explain why the Howard government has been left relatively unscathed by its membership of the Coalition of the Willing in Iraq and, until recently, the Coalition of the Unwilling on climate change.

Sally Warhaft, Australian editor of *The Monthly*

You will become a political penguin on a smaller and smaller ice floe that is drifting out to sea. Goodbye, my little friend.

Arnold Schwarzenegger, American-Austrian Republican Governor of California, former actor and bodybuilder about politicians who don't act to decrease greenhouse gas emissions

If they don't act, we will. Shame on them but we cannot sit around and watch our environment deteriorate and put this world in jeopardy.

Michael Bloomberg, American businessman and New York City mayor about politicians who don't act to decrease greenhouse gas emissions

I have to admit that, until recently, I was somewhat wary of the warming debate. I believe it is now our responsibility to take the lead on this issue.

Rupert Murdoch, Australian-American businessman, in a 2007 speech

Twelve months ago when I told the kids to turn off the lights I was an old grouch. Now I'm an environmental warrior.

Richard Glover, Australian journalist and ABC broadcaster, in 2007

The Chinese expression for crisis consists of two characters side by side. The first symbol means danger. The second symbol means opportunity. I would like to discuss both the danger and the opportunity here today.

Al Gore, former American Democrat vice president and 2007 Nobel Peace Prize winner, to a 2007 American Senate Committee

One of the things I learned from my political career about the climate crisis is that the resistance to change is so deep, the denial is so strong and the financial interests threatened by some of the necessary changes are so powerful, that it is foolish to expect that any political leaders will be able to make speeches and rally people to support some massive legislative action.

Al Gore

Famous Phrase: 'an inconvenient truth'

There's no longer any debate in the scientific community about this. But the political systems around the world have held this at arm's length because it's an inconvenient truth, because they don't want to accept that it's a moral imperative.

Al Gore

Communication

Writers, like teeth, are divided into incisors and grinders.

Walter Bagehot (1826–1877), British journalist and economist

Many attempts to communicate are nullified by saying too much.

Robert Greenleef (1904–1990), American management researcher

Some books are undeservedly forgotten; none are undeservedly remembered.

W.H. Auden (1907–1973), British poet

We're a voicemail company not an email company.

Brad Keeling, former Australian One.Tel marketing executive about an aspect of the failed company's communication policy

Television has made dictatorship impossible, but democracy unbearable.

Shimon Peres, Israeli president

I talk and talk and talk, and I haven't taught people in fifty years what my father taught me by example in one week.

Mario Cuomo, American Democrat politician and former New York City mayor

Some editors are failed writers, but so are most writers.

T.S. Eliot (1888–1965), British poet

What is written without effort is, in general, read without pleasure.

Samuel Johnson (1709–1784), British writer and lexicographer

To write one's memoirs is to speak ill of everybody except oneself.

Marshal Petain (1856–1941), French politician

Without credible communication, and a lot of it, employee hearts and minds are never captured.

John Kotter, American management academic and author of *Leading Change*

Words ought to be a little wild for they are the assault of the thoughts on the unthinking.

John Maynard Keynes (1883–1946), British economist

Words are, of course, the most powerful drug used by mankind.

Rudyard Kipling (1865–1936), English writer

The surest way to make a monkey of a man is to quote him.

Robert Benchley (1889–1945), American writer

English is the perfect language for preachers because it allows you to talk until you think of what to say.

Garrison Keillor, American writer

I remind myself every morning: Nothing I say this day will teach me anything. So if I'm going to learn, I must do it by listening.

Larry King, American broadcaster

A memorandum is written not to inform the reader but to protect the writer.

Dean Acheson (1893–1971), American secretary of state

Men communicate to obtain information, establish their status, and show independence. Women communicate to create relationships, encourage interaction, and exchange feelings.

Judy B. Rosener, American business management commentator and author

Video conferencing will save us $US150 million in travel expenses next year. I know that for a fact because I've already taken the budget away from everyone.

John Chambers, American, Cisco Systems chairman and CEO

A large part of communications skills, which people forget, is listening.

John Chambers

A quotation is what a speaker wants to say—unlike a soundbite which is all that an interviewer allows you to say.

Tony Benn, former British Labour minister

He knew the precise psychological moment when to say nothing.

Oscar Wilde (1854–1900), Irish writer

Listen first, speak last.

Peter Drucker (1909–2005), American-Austrian management academic and writer

Communication is not saying something, communication is being heard.

Peter Drucker

Knowing how a typewriter works does not make you a writer.

Peter Drucker

The most important thing in communication is hearing what isn't said.

Peter Drucker

The unspoken word is capital. We can invest it or we can squander it.

Mark Twain (1835–1910), American writer

> The right word may be effective, but no word was ever as effective as a rightly timed pause.
>
> Mark Twain

Silence is often a good policy on some subjects in politics, but silence is regarded as a sort of sin now, and it has to be filled with a lot of gossip and sound bites.

Douglas Hurd, former British Conservative foreign secretary

The great enemy of clear language is insincerity. When there is a gap between one's real and one's declared aims, one turns as it were instinctively to long words and exhausted idioms, like a cuttlefish squirting out ink.

George Orwell (1903–1950), British writer

Consumers and customers

The entire world economy rests on the consumer; if he ever stops spending money he doesn't have on things he doesn't need—we're done for.

Bill Bonner, American economist and writer

Ms Market, we have found, is like a woman—coy, changeable and contemptuous of our efforts to understand her. We will never fathom what moves her; we might as well be a golden retriever trying to decipher the Tokyo train schedules.

Bill Bonner

When you stop talking, you've lost your customer. When you turn your back, you've lost her.

Estee Lauder (1907–2004), American businesswoman

Our belief was that if we kept putting great products in front of customers, they would continue to open their wallets.

Steve Jobs, American businessman and founder of Apple Computers

Once again, we come to the Holiday Season, a deeply religious time that each of us observes, in his own way, by going to the mall of his choice.

Dave Barry, American comedian

There is only one boss. The customer. And he can fire everybody in the company from the chairman down, simply by spending his money somewhere else.

Sam Walton (1918–1992), American businessman and Wal-Mart founder

These days, you can't succeed as a company if you're consumer-led—because, in a world so full of so much constant change, consumers can't anticipate the next big thing. Companies should be idea-led and consumer-informed.

Douglas Atkin, American advertising executive and author

The consumer isn't a moron. She is your wife.

David Ogilvy (1911–1999), American-English advertising executive

The unique take that we've had is tapping our customers as a source of ideas for the business, recognising that the customers are the people who are most likely to be able to innovate on behalf of the business.

Remo Giuffre, Australian businessman and founder of REMO General Store

Your most unhappy customers are your greatest source of learning.

Bill Gates, American, Microsoft co-founder and *Forbes* richest man in the world since 1995

The public is never wrong.

Adolph Zukor (1873–1976), American founder of Paramount Pictures

When you preach to the choir, you get a great reception: but your back is to the congregation.

John Faulkner, Australian federal Labor senator

In our rich consumers' civilization we spin cocoons around ourselves and get possessed by our possessions.

Max Lerner (1902–1992), American journalist

A consumer is a shopper who is sore about something.

Harold Coffin (1905–1981), American writer

In today's increasingly philanthropic climate, expect conspicuous self-indulgence to go straight to the social guillotine. The globally conscious consumer regards altruistic activities as a necessary part of self-improvement.

Faith Popcorn, American futurist, 2007 prediction

Statistics suggest that when customers complain, business owners and managers ought to get excited about it. The complaining customer represents a huge opportunity for more business.

Zig Ziglar, American motivational writer and speaker

The advertisement succeeded when it discovered, defined, and persuaded a new community of consumers.

Daniel J. Boorstin (1914–2004), American historian, professor, attorney, and writer

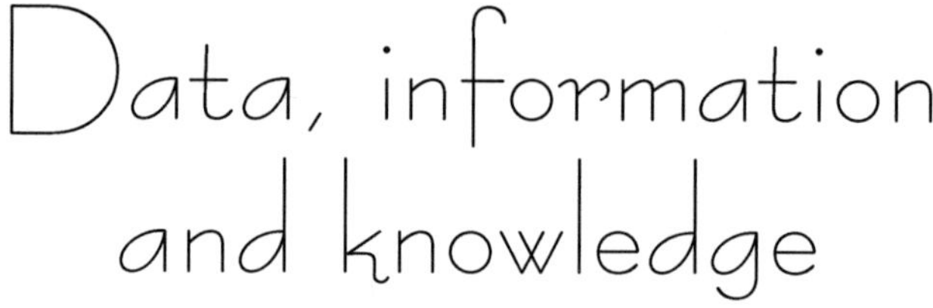

The trouble with the information revolution is that there is way too much information.

Mike Carlton, Australian broadcaster, journalist and newspaper columnist

Extraordinary claims require extraordinary evidence.

Carl Sagan (1934–1996), American scientist and writer

We are drowning in information but starved for knowledge.
John Naisbitt, American business writer and researcher

Excessive word count and worthless details are making it harder for people to extract useful information. The more you say, the more people tune out your message.
Jakob Nielsen, American-Danish web usability expert

Stealing from one author is plagiarism; stealing from three authors is research.
Sir Owen Dixon (1886–1972), Australian judge and diplomat

The other characteristic of knowledge is that for a person to have a piece of knowledge it is assumed that they understand it.
Peter Morris, Australian businessman

Luck always follows the prepared mind.
Jim Rogers, American investor and co-founder with George Soros of the Quantum Fund

If you file your wastepaper basket for 50 years, you have a public library.
Tony Benn, former British Labour minister

Information is a beacon, a cudgel, an olive branch, a deterrent, depending on who wields it and how.
Steven D. Levitt and Stephen J. Dubner, American authors of *Freakonomics*

The fewer data needed, the better the information. And an overload of information, that is, anything much beyond what is truly needed, leads to information blackout. It does not enrich, but impoverishes.

Peter Drucker (1909–2005), American-Austrian management academic and writer

Information is the oxygen of the modern age. It seeps through the walls topped by barbed wire, it wafts across the electrified borders.

Ronald Reagan (1911–2004), American president

His nickname was 'Trevor the Shredder', because after a board meeting there were always documents he wanted shredded.

Glenn Barry, an American executive about former Consolidated Press executive Trevor Kennedy's approach to record-keeping

Famous Phrase: '57 channels and nothing on'

There's fifty-seven channels and nothin' on.

Bruce Springsteen, American singer and songwriter, from his 1992 song about the trappings of a bourgeois life

Deals, winners and losers

It's hard to feel powerful when you're sucking on a Paddlepop.

Rob Stirling, Australian business executive about the negotiating tactics of Jodee Rich, the founder of One.Tel

All government, indeed every human benefit and enjoyment, every virtue and every prudent act, is founded on compromise.

Edmund Burke (1729–1797), British politician and philosopher

Win/Win is a frame of mind and heart that constantly seeks mutual benefit in all human interactions.

Steven Covey, American author of *The Seven Habits of Highly Effective People*

It's a well-known proposition that you know who's going to win negotiation: it's he who pauses the longest.

Robert Holmes a Court (1937–1990), Australian businessman

Winning is not enough. All others must lose.

Larry Ellison, American business executive and co-founder of Oracle Corporation

The important thing in life is not the victory but the contest; the essential thing is not to have won but to have fought well.

Baron Pierre de Coubertin (1863–1937), founder of the modern Olympics

Leverage is having something the other guy wants.

Donald Trump, American businessman

Deals are my art form. Other people paint beautifully on canvas or write wonderful poetry. I like making deals, preferably big deals. That's how I get my kicks.

Donald Trump

I don't make deals for the money. I've got enough, much more than I'll ever need. I do it to do it.

Donald Trump

One of the things I learnt when I was negotiating was that until I changed myself I could not change others.

Nelson Mandela, former South African president, said in 2000

An agreement between two men to do what both agree is wrong.

Lord Edward Cecil (1867–1918), British civil servant, definition of a compromise

The market economy is all about winners and losers. You can't have winners without losers. Without losers, you don't have winners.

Scott McNealy, American, co-founder and former Sun Microsystems CEO

To win you have to risk loss.

Jean-Claude Killy, French professional skier and IOC member

Never underestimate the other guy.

Jack Welch, American, former General Electric CEO

If there's one characteristic all winners share, it's that they care more than anyone else.

Jack Welch

There are not fifty ways of fighting, there's only one, and that's to win.

Andre Malraux (1901–1976), French politician and writer

Labor has had plenty of practice at losing. That doesn't make us 'good losers'.

John Faulkner, Australian federal Labor senator

Finishing second in the Olympics gets you silver. Finishing second in politics gets you oblivion.

Richard Nixon (1913–1994), American president

Winning is everything. The only ones who remember when you come second are your wife and your dog.

Damon Hill, British racing driver

The winner is the chef who takes the same ingredients as everyone else and produces the best results.

Edward de Bono, Maltese-British psychologist and writer

Losers have meetings, winners have parties.

Sam Chisolm, Australian, former Channel Nine and BSkyB executive

I would say that the quality of each man's life is the full measure of that man's personal commitment to excellence and to victory—whether it be football, whether it be business, whether it be politics or government.

Vince Lombardi (1913–1970), American football coach

We see plenty of opportunities in things that Google might or might not do. If you read the newspapers today, other than curing cancer, Google will do everything.

Steve Ballmer, American, Microsoft CEO

Losers spend time explaining why they lost. Losers spend their lives thinking about what they're going to do. They rarely enjoy doing what they're doing.

Dr Eric Berne (1910–1970), Canadian psychiatrist

It must be a peace without victory ... Victory would mean peace forced upon the losers, a victor's terms imposed upon the vanquished. It would be accepted in humiliation, under duress, at an intolerable sacrifice, and would leave a sting, a resentment, a bitter memory upon which the terms of peace would rest, not permanently, but only as upon quicksand.

Woodrow Wilson (1856–1924), American president

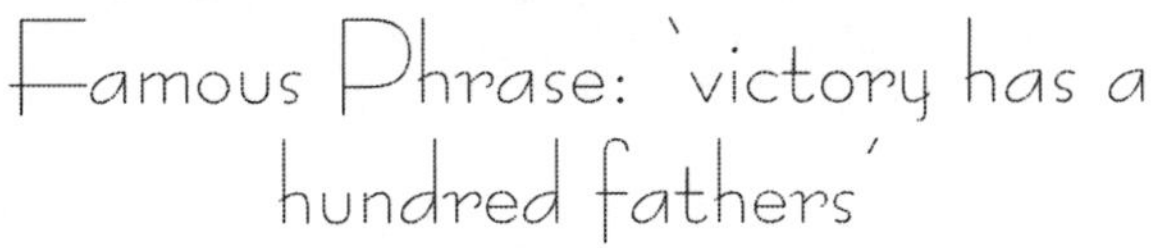

Famous Phrase: 'victory has a hundred fathers'

Victory has a hundred fathers, but no-one wants to recognise defeat as his own.

Count Galeazzo Ciano (1903–1944), Italian fascist politician, often quoted as 'Victory has a hundred fathers, but defeat is an orphan'

Democracy and despots

Democracy means government by discussion, but it is only effective if you can stop people talking.

Clement Attlee (1883–1967), British prime minister

Those who would give up essential liberty to purchase a little temporary safety, deserve neither liberty nor safety.

Benjamin Franklin (1706–1790), American politician and 'founding father'

In a democracy everybody has a right to be represented, including the jerks.

Chris Patten, former British Conservative politician

Don't get mad. Don't get even. Just get elected, then get even.

James Carville, American political consultant most widely known for his advice to Bill Clinton during 1992 presidential campaign

The American people have spoken—but it's going to take a little while to determine exactly what they said.

Bill Clinton, former American president about the 2000 American presidential results

I always knew that some day I would once again feel the grass under my feet and walk in the sunshine as a free man.

Nelson Mandela, former South African president

What is freedom of expression? Without the freedom to offend, it ceases to exist.

Salman Rushdie, British-Indian writer who had a 'fatwa' issued by then Iranian leader, Ayatollah Khomeini, following the 1988 publication of *The Satanic Verses*

The supremacist ideology of the Bush Administration stands in opposition to the principles of an open society, which recognise that people have different views and that nobody is in possession of the ultimate truth.

George Soros, American-Hungarian investor and co-founder of the Quantum Group of Funds

A society that puts equality before freedom will get neither. A society that puts freedom before equality will get a high degree of both.

Milton Friedman (1912–2006), American economist

Through talk, we tamed kings, restrained tyrants, averted revolution.

Tony Benn, former British Labour minister

I disapprove of what you say, but I will defend to the death your right to say it.

Evelyn Beatrice Hall (1868–1919), British writer who wrote under the psuedonym S.G. Tallentyre. This quote is often attributed to Voltaire but it is Hall's description of Voltaire's beliefs.

Those who can make you believe absurdities can make you commit atrocities.

Voltaire (1694–1778), French philosopher and writer

My job is not to represent Washington to you, but to represent you to Washington.

Barack Obama, American Democrat senator and 2008 presidential candidate

After leaving the Kremlin ... my conscience was clear. The promise I gave the people when I started the process of *perestroika* was kept: I gave them freedom.

Mikhail Gorbachev, former leader of the Soviet Union

The guilt of Stalin and his immediate entourage before the Party and the people for the mass repressions and lawlessness they committed is enormous and unforgivable.

Mikhail Gorbachev

Liberty sets the mind free, fosters independence and unorthodox thinking and ideas. But it does not offer instant prosperity or happiness and wealth to everyone.

Boris Yeltsin (1931–2007), Russian president

You can build a throne with bayonets, but you can't sit on it for long.

Boris Yeltsin

It's very different living in academia in Oxford. We called someone vicious in the *Times Literary Supplement*. We didn't know what vicious was.

Aung San Suu Kyi, Burmese politician who won the 1990 democratic election but was arrested following a military coup and has been under house arrest since

The shape of Africa resembles a revolver, and the Congo is the trigger.

Frantz Fanon (1925–1961), French writer

A single death is a tragedy, a million deaths is a statistic.

Joseph Stalin (1878–1953), Soviet leader

You have not converted a man because you have silenced him.

John Morley (1838–1923), British Liberal politician

I will make you shorter by the head.

Queen Elizabeth I of England and Ireland (1533–1603) to her advisers who opposed her actions to Mary Queen of Scots

Let us not be deceived—we are today in the midst of a cold war.

Bernard Baruch (1870–1965), American presidential adviser and investor (the phrase 'cold war' was suggested to him by H.B. Swope, *New York World* editor)

Diplomacy and foreign affairs

We're eyeball to eyeball, and I think the other fellow just blinked.

Dean Rusk (1909–1994), American Democrat secretary of state during the 1962 Cuban missile crisis

The first requirement of a statesman is that he be dull.

Dean Acheson (1893–1971), American Democrat secretary of state

Living next to you is in some ways like sleeping with an elephant. No matter how friendly and even–tempered the beast, one is affected by every twitch and grunt.

Pierre Trudeau (1919–2000), Canadian prime minister, about Canada's overbearing southern neighbour

The chief distinction of a diplomat is that he can say no in such a way that it sounds like yes.

Lester Pearson (1897–1972), Canadian Liberal prime minister

We hear the Secretary of State boasting of his brinkmanship—the art of bringing us to the edge of the abyss.

Adlai Stevenson (1900–1965), American Democrat politician about then Secretary of State John Foster Dulles

Cricket civilises people and creates good gentlemen. I want everyone to play cricket in Zimbabwe; I want ours to be a nation of gentlemen.

Robert Mugabe, Zimbabwean president

You can put up a sign on the door, 'beware of the dog', without having a dog.

Hans Blix, Swedish diplomat and head of the UN's Monitoring, Verification and Inspection Commission tasked with finding weapons of mass destruction in Iraq in 2002–2003

Every American sleeps better in his bed because he knows that if his country is attacked, New Zealand will come to his defence.

Keith Holyoake (1904–1983), New Zealand prime minister, about the ANZUS Treaty

Wherever the American is resisting aggression, wherever the United States or the United Kingdom is resisting aggression, or any other country is seeking to ensure that there will be a chance for free expression, then we'll go waltzing Matilda with you.

John Gorton (1911–2002), Australian prime minister

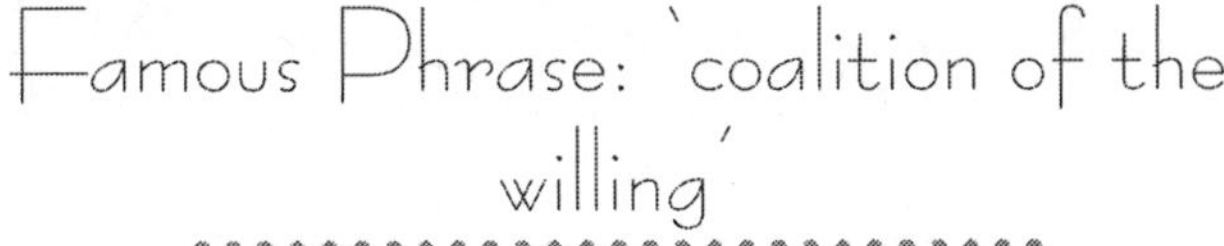

Famous Phrase: 'coalition of the willing'

If the collective will of the world is strong, we can achieve disarmament peacefully. However, should he choose not to disarm, the United States will lead a coalition of the willing to disarm him.

George W. Bush, American president, speech on 20 November 2002 about the threat of Saddam Hussein's 'weapons of mass destruction'

Economics and economists

The purpose of astrology is to make economic forecasting seem reasonable.

John Kenneth Galbraith (1908–2006), American-Canadian economist

There is an old saying, or should be, that it is a wise economist who recognises the scope of his own generalisations.

John Kenneth Galbraith

Sometimes I wonder if our central bank is just going to print money until we run out of trees.

Jim Rogers, American investor and co-founder with George Soros of the Quantum Fund

The first lesson of economics is scarcity: there is never enough of anything to satisfy all those who want it. The first lesson of politics is to disregard the first lesson of economics.

Thomas Sowell, American economist

Christmas is a time when kids tell Santa what they want and adults pay for it. Deficits are when adults tell the government what they want and their kids pay for it.

Richard Lamm, former American Democrat politician

Economists are the great imperialists of the social sciences.

Gardner Ackley (1915–1998), American economist

There is only one social responsibility of business—to use its resources and engage in activities designed to increase its profits without deception or fraud.

Milton Friedman (1912–2006), American economist

An economist is a man who states the obvious in terms of the incomprehensible.

Alfred A. Knopf (1892–1984), American book publisher

A man can be forgiven a lot if he can quote Shakespeare in an economic crisis.

Prince Philip, Queen Elizabeth II's husband

To those critics who are so pessimistic about our economy, I say, don't be economic girlie men!

Arnold Schwarzenegger, American-Austrian Republican Governor of California, former actor and bodybuilder

It would not be altogether inappropriate to characterise the post-war economy as a 'milk bar' economy.

Sir Douglas Copland (1894–1971), Australian economist

Economists think the poor need them to tell them that they are poor.

Peter Drucker (1909–2005), American-Austrian management academic and writer

If economists were any good at business, they would be rich men instead of advisers to rich men.

Kirk Kerkorian, American businessman and father of the mega-resort

Economics are the method; the object is to change the soul.

Margaret Thatcher, former British prime minister

Unfortunately monetarism, like Marxism, suffered the only fate that for a theory is worse than death: it was put into practice.

Ian Gilmour (1926–2007), British Conservative politician and peer

The market is not an invention of capitalism. It has existed for centuries. It is an invention of civilisation.

Mikhail Gorbachev, last Soviet president

If I'd wanted to exercise, I'd have never become an economist.

President Josiah Bartlet from fictional television series, *The West Wing*

Where money for projects has not been found, we will print it.

Robert Mugabe, Zimbabwean president, about meeting a money shortfall for municipal projects (despite the annual inflation rate being more than 4500 per cent)

The free lunch has still to be invented.

Alan Greenspan, American economist and former chairman of the board of governors of the Federal Reserve

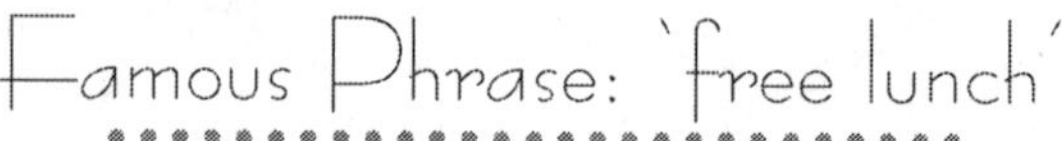

There's no such thing as a free lunch.

Originally coined by American writer Robert Heinlein as 'There ain't no such thing as a free lunch' (frequently shortened to the acronym TANSTAAFL) in his 1966 novel, *The Moon is a Harsh Mistress*, but popularised by and frequently attributed to Milton Friedman

An organisation's ability to learn, and translate that learning into action rapidly, is the ultimate competitive advantage.

Jack Welch, American, former General Electric CEO

I've learned that mistakes can often be as good a teacher as success.

Jack Welch

Education is a method by which one acquires a higher grade of prejudices.

Laurence J. Peter (1919–1990), Canadian academic

I am still learning.

Michelangelo (1475–1564), Italian sculptor, artist, architect and engineer

A university should be a place of light, of liberty and of learning.

Benjamin Disraeli (1804–1881), British prime minister

Education has failed in a very serious way to convey the most important lesson science can teach: skepticism.

David Suzuki, Canadian scientist and environmental activist

If you think that education is expensive, try ignorance.

Derek Bok, American, former Harvard University president

There is only one thing that can kill the movies, and that is education.

Will Rogers (1879–1935), American actor and writer

People with a high level of personal mastery live in a continual learning mode. They never 'arrive'.

Peter Senge, American management academic

People create their own success by learning what they need to learn and then by practicing it until they become proficient at it.

Brian Tracy, American sales and management self-help author

You can get used to being a player without being a winner. There's a big difference between the two. So I became interested in transforming players into winners.

Alan G. Lafley, American business executive and Proctor & Gamble executive director

If you make the most of [education], you study hard, you do your homework, and you make an effort to be smart, you can do well. If you don't, you get stuck in Iraq.

John Kerry, American Democrat politician during the 2004 American presidential campaign

Effort, efficiency and effectiveness

Effort is only effort when it begins to hurt.

José Ortega y Gasset (1883–1955), Spanish philosopher

You have to put in many, many, many tiny efforts that nobody sees or appreciates before you achieve anything worthwhile.

Brian Tracy, American sales and management self-help author

Efficiency is doing things right. Effectiveness is doing the right thing.

Zig Ziglar, American motivational writer and speaker

I have never encountered an executive who remains effective while tackling more than two tasks at once.

Peter Drucker (1909–2005), American-Austrian management academic and writer

You remind me of a person on a step exercise machine, always going up but never getting anywhere.

Barbara Amiel, British-American wife of Conrad Black (former financier and newspaper magnate), a parting insult to a former friend

Frazzing—frantic, ineffective multi-tasking, typically with the delusion that you are getting a lot done. The quality of the work, however, is poor.

Edward Hallowell, American psychiatrist and author

Fantastic things happen—to the way we feel, to the way we make other people feel. All this simply by using positive words.

Leo Buscaglia (1924–1998), American-Italian teacher and writer

Our spirit of enjoyment was stronger than our spirit of sacrifice. We wanted to have more than we wanted to give. We tried to spare effort, and met disaster.

Henri Philippe Pétain (1856–1951), French general

Basically, I have no place in organised politics. By coming to the British Parliament, I've allowed the people to sacrifice me at the top and let go the more effective job I should be doing at the bottom.

Bernadette Devlin, Irish politician

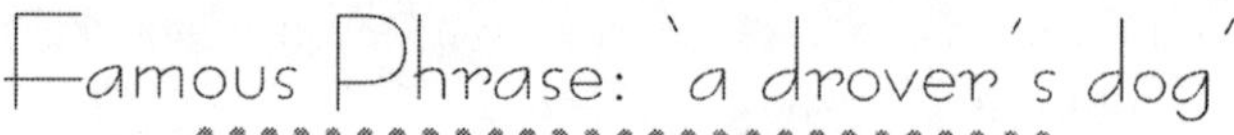

I am not convinced the Labor Party could not win under my leadership. I believe a drover's dog could lead the Labor Party to victory the way the country is.

Bill Hayden, former Australian Labor Party leader after his replacement by Bob Hawke who subsequently lead the party to victory in the 1983 federal election

Equality/inequality

It still staggers me that for the first ten years of my life, I existed under the Flora and Fauna Act of NSW.

Linda Burney, indigenous Australian NSW Labor politician

All that has changed today is white men have replaced bullets and poisoned flour with a more sophisticated form of discrimination to keep Aboriginals oppressed and fragmented.

Neville Bonner (1922–1999), Australian politician, first Aboriginal Member of Parliament

I was so angry because they were denying they had done anything wrong, denying that a whole generation was stolen.

Catherine Freeman, Australian Olympic athlete, in the aftermath of the *Bringing Them Home: Stolen Children* report, which investigated the impact of the practice of taking Aboriginal children from their parents and placing them in institutions or with white families

We now in the United States have more security guards for the rich than we have police services for the poor districts. If you're looking for personal security, far better to move to the suburbs than to pay taxes in New York.

John Kenneth Galbraith (1908–2006), American-Canadian economist

The Gypsies are a litmus test not of democracy but of a civil society.

Vaclav Havel, former Czech Republic president

If you're born in America with a black skin, you're born in prison.

Malcolm X (1925–1965), American civil rights campaigner

Not only did we play the race card, we played it from the bottom of the deck.

Robert Shapiro, American defence lawyer for O.J. Simpson

Remember the good old times of black and white TV? It was mainly white.

Whoopi Goldberg, American actor

You can be up to your boobies in white satin, with gardenias in your hair and no sugar cane for miles, but you can still be working on a plantation.

Billie Holliday (1915–1959), American jazz singer

I detest racialism because I regard it as a barbaric thing, whether it comes from a black man or a white man.

Nelson Mandela, former South African president

The Republicans don't care about the working poor—they don't know any.

James Carville, American political consultant most widely known for his advice to Bill Clinton during the 1992 presidential campaign

Famous Phrase: 'a place called hope'

I end tonight where it all began for me: I still believe in a place called Hope.

Bill Clinton, former American Democrat president, a play on words based on the name of his birthplace (Hope, Arkansas)

Generation gap generalisations

Nothing so dates a man as to decry the younger generation.

Adlai Stevenson (1900–1965), American Democrat politician

Today's twentysomething Generation Ys will one day be sixtysomething—and it's safe to say they'll look and act a little differently then, even though they'll still be called Generation Y. So don't confuse the current age or life stage (which will change) with the label (which won't).

Mark McCrindle, Australian social researcher and writer

From a hype perspective, baby boomers are old news because they turn 60 this year.

Mark McCrindle

Generation Y has no spending power.

Mark McCrindle

Not only do Xers have excellent dentures (a consequence of the introduction of fluoride into the water during their childhood) but they have meekly accepted the fact that they have to fork out for tertiary education whereas much of the baby boomer generation got their degrees for free!

Bernard Salt, Australian demographer and writer

Boomer logic was that you start off with crap and you build to quality.

Bernard Salt

Ys are taken with the idea of starting at say the middle, flitting back to the beginning, and then perhaps sampling the end.

Bernard Salt

Generation Y has been brought up to be always on. It's not the internet for them, it's life. It's not a mobile phone, it's communication.

Dion Appel, Australian businessman

They think it's their right to have what they want, they're brash and naive and they can really be like spoilt kids who say 'I want a pony now, I've got four ponies at home but I want another one and I want it now'. You don't want that at work.

Jo Nagle, Australian, chief executive of marketing company Let's Launch

These kids are smart ... but I'd as soon take a python to bed as hire one.

Ned Dewey, American investor and Harvard Business School graduate about recent graduates

Many businesses have not yet shed the outdated view that the mature market is made up of stingy old-timers set in their ways. Unless you are in the business of prescription drugs or retirement homes ... why bother.

The Economist, an English-language news and current affairs magazine, August 2002

I think X and Y will be many things that the baby boomers will never be. They have more choice, they have more comfort, they are more confident.

Geoff Morgan, Australian, co-founder of recruitment company Talent2

It's time to bump these Baby Bleaters and their ceaseless cries for more milk.

Ryan Heath, Australian Gen Y political media adviser and author of *Please Just F* Off, It's Our Turn Now*

Boomer women have doubled their consumption of alcohol in the past 10 years. The same goes for overseas travel. Generation Y are simply not as profitable as the boomer generation.

Gill Walker, Australian, director and founder of Evergreen Marketing Communications

Famous Phrase: 'one for the country'

One for your husband, one for your wife, one for your country. You go home and do your patriotic duty.

Peter Costello, Australian Treasurer, in 2005 about the need to lift the birth rate to pay for the forecast cost of baby boomers' retirement

High moral ground

There are not enough jails, not enough policemen, not enough courts to enforce a law not supported by the people.

Hubert Humphrey (1911–1978), American Democrat politician

Compassion is not weakness, and concern for the unfortunate is not socialism.

Hubert Humphrey

Sacred cows make the tastiest hamburgers.

Abbie Hoffman (1936–1989), American left wing political activist and co-founder of the Yippies (Youth International Party)

There's a very thin line between dying for Ireland and killing for Ireland.

John Hume, Northern Irish politician and co-recipient of the 1998 Nobel Peace Prize

The political and commercial morals of the United States are not merely food for laughter, they are an entire banquet.

Mark Twain (1835–1910), American writer

Always do the right thing. This will gratify some people and astonish the rest.

Mark Twain

Values are and should be the ultimate test.

Peter Drucker (1909–2005), American-Austrian management academic and writer

These are not grounds for impeachment. These are grounds for divorce.

Maureen Dowd, American, *New York Times* columnist about the Monica Lewinsky scandal during Bill Clinton's presidency

A president's hardest task is not to do what is right, but to know what is right.

Lyndon Baines Johnson (1908–1973), American Democrat president

If you can manipulate news, a judge can manipulate the law. A smart lawyer can keep a killer out of jail, a smart accountant can keep a thief from paying taxes, a smart reporter could ruin your reputation—unfairly.

Mario Cuomo, American Democrat politician and former New York City mayor

I am against government by crony.

Harold L. Ickes (1874–1952), American Democrat politician

I want to work for a company that contributes to and is part of the community. I want something not just to invest in. I want something to believe in.

Dame Anita Roddick (1942–2007), British businesswoman and founder of The Body Shop

Go to where the silence is and say something.

Amy Goodman, American journalist, following an award for her coverage of 1991 East Timor massacre

Few trends could so thoroughly undermine the very foundations of our free society as the acceptance by corporate officials of a social responsibility other than to make as much money for their stockholders as possible.

Milton Friedman (1912–2004), American economist

Morality is simply the attitude we adopt towards people we personally dislike.

Oscar Wilde (1854–1900), Irish writer

Famous Phrase: 'life isn't meant to be easy'

Life is not meant to be easy, my child; but take courage: it can be delightful.

George Bernard Shaw (1856–1950), Irish writer. This phrase was made famous in Australia when former prime minister Malcolm Fraser used it.

Image, ideas and innovation

Political image is like mixing cement. When it's wet, you can move it around and shape it, but at some point it hardens and there's almost nothing you can do to reshape it.

Walter Mondale, former American Democrat vice president

Once we were larrikins with a taste of defiance; now we are lapdogs with a thirst for conformity.

Bob Brown, Australian Greens senator, about the Australian–American relationship

There is only one step from the sublime to the ridiculous.

Napoleon I (1769–1821), French military leader and emperor

I find it rather easy to portray a businessman. Being bland, rather cruel, and incompetent comes naturally to me.

John Cleese, British actor and comedian

Microsoft is now talking about the digital nervous system. I guess I would be nervous if my system was built on their technology, too.

Scott McNealy, American, co-founder and former Sun Microsystems CEO

Ridiculous yachts and private planes and big limousines won't make people enjoy life more, and it sends out terrible messages to the people who work for them. It would be so much better if that money was spent in Africa—and it's about getting a balance.

Sir Richard Branson, British businessman and founder of the Virgin Group

I never, ever thought of myself as a businessman. I was interested in creating things I would be proud of.

Sir Richard Branson

Our company has, indeed, stumbled onto some of its new products. But never forget that you can only stumble if you're moving.

Richard P. Carlton, American, former 3M vice president

At Microsoft there are lots of brilliant ideas but the image is that they all come from the top—I'm afraid that's not quite right.

Bill Gates, American, Microsoft co-founder and Forbes richest man in the world since 1995

Think for yourself and let others enjoy the privilege of doing so too.

Voltaire (1694–1778), French philosopher and writer

To turn really interesting ideas and fledgling technologies into a company that can continue to innovate for years, it requires a lot of disciplines.

Steve Jobs, American businessman and founder of Apple Computers

It's really hard to design products by focus groups. A lot of times, people don't know what they want until you show it to them.

Steve Jobs

Innovation has nothing to do with how many R&D dollars you have. When Apple came up with the Mac, IBM was spending at least 100 times more on R&D. It's not about money. It's about the people you have, how you're led, and how much you get it.

Steve Jobs

Innovation distinguishes between a leader and a follower.

Steve Jobs

The enemy of the conventional wisdom is not ideas but the march of events.

John Kenneth Galbraith (1908–2006), American-Canadian economist

Failure is our most important product.

Robert W. Johnson II (1893–1968), American, Johnson & Johnson CEO

Do not go where the path may lead, go instead where there is no path and leave a trail.

Ralph Waldo Emerson (1803–1882), American writer

The point is not to 'push the envelope' or to 'think outside the box'. The point is to rip up the envelope and to burn the box.

Tom Peters, American management consultant

You've got to be careful to balance that encouragement of creativity with respect for the bean counters.

Remo Giuffre, Australian businessman and founder of REMO General Store

I think there is a world market for about five computers.

Thomas J. Watson (1874–1956), American, IBM CEO, comment from 1945

Who the hell wants to hear actors talk?

Henry Warner (1881–1958), Polish-American, co-founder of Warner Brothers, about the advent of talking pictures

There is no reason for any individual to have a computer in his home.

Ken Olson, American business executive and Digital Equipment Corporation president, comment from 1977

It's a stupid fad and will be gone in three years.

Carl Zeiss (1816–1888), German lens maker and businessman about the Kodak Brownie in 1888

All men's gains are the fruit of venturing.

Herodotus (484–425 BC), Greek historian

Innovation: the art of translating a vision into reality.

Dr Robin John Batterham, Australian government chief scientist

We've got a story to tell that isn't just against something but is for something.

Barack Obama, American Democrat senator and 2008 presidential candidate

Ideas are like rabbits. You get a couple, learn how to look after them, and pretty soon you have a dozen.

John Steinbeck (1902–1968), American writer

Every organisation needs one core competence: innovation.

Peter Drucker (1909–2005), American-Austrian management academic and writer

Intelligence

Brains are becoming the core of organisations—other activities can be contracted out.

Charles Handy, British-Irish philosopher and management writer

Emotional intelligence—the ability to manage ourselves and our relationships effectively—consists of four fundamental capabilities: self-awareness, self-management, social awareness, and social skill.

Daniel Goleman, American psychologist and writer

The most difficult subjects can be explained to the most slow-witted man if he has not formed any idea of them already; but the simplest thing cannot be made clear to the most intelligent man if he is firmly persuaded that he knows already, without a shadow of doubt, what is laid before him.

Leo Tolstoy (1828–1910), Russian writer

Wealth, in even the most improbable cases, manages to convey the aspect of intelligence.

John Kenneth Galbraith (1908–2006), American-Canadian economist

A TV programme can never be worse than its viewers; for the more stupid it is, the more stupid they are to watch it.

Clive James, ex-patriate Australian writer

I use not only all the brains I have but all I can borrow.

Woodrow Wilson (1856–1924), American president

The test of a first-rate intelligence is the ability to hold two opposed ideas in the mind at the same time, and still retain the ability to function.

F. Scott Fitzgerald (1896–1940), American writer

Lord Birkenhead is very clever but sometimes his brains go to his head.

Margot Asquith (1864–1945), British socialite and wife of prime minister Herbert Asquith

No one in this world, so far as I know—and I have searched the records for years, and employed agents to help me—has ever lost money by underestimating the intelligence of the great masses of the plain people.

H.L. Mencken (1880–1956), American journalist

Thinking is the hardest work there is, which is probably the reason so few engage in it.

Henry Ford (1863–1947), American, founder of the Ford Motor Company

Give me a smart idiot before a stupid genius any day.

Samuel Goldwyn (1882–1974), Polish-American film producer

Keep doing what you've been doing and you will keep getting what you've been getting!

Jackie B. Cooper (1939–2001), American car industry trainer

Many highly intelligent people are poor thinkers. Many people of average intelligence are skilled thinkers. The power of a car is separate from the way a car is driven.

Edward de Bono, Maltese-British psychologist and writer

Progress comes from the intelligent use of experience.

Elbert Hubbard (1856–1915), American writer

Let us be thankful for the fools. But for them the rest of us could not succeed.

Mark Twain (1835–1910), American writer

Intelligence will seize the immediate meaning in a situation and evaluate it.

Richard Hofstadter (1916–1970), American historian

Having intelligence is not as important as knowing when to use it, just as having a hoe is not as important as knowing when to plant.

Chinese proverb

I happen to feel that the degree of a person's intelligence is directly reflected by the number of conflicting attitudes she can bring to bear on the same topic.

Lisa Alther, American novelist

Who's in charge of the clattering train?

Lord Beaverbrook (1879–1964), Canadian-British newspaper owner and politician, would say this when he entered one of his newsrooms

When you confront a problem you begin to solve it.

Rudy Giuliani, American, former New York City mayor, Republican 2008 presidential candidate. Giuliani's popularity was in decline until the terrorist attacks of September 11 when he displayed reassuring leadership.

Leaders need to be optimists. Their vision is beyond the present.

Rudy Giuliani

Managers have their eyes on the bottom line; leaders have their eyes on the horizon.

Warren Bennis, American management writer and consultant

Leaders learn by leading, and they learn best by leading in the face of obstacles. As the weather shapes mountains, problems shape leaders.

Warren Bennis

Failing leaders are usually over-managed and under-led.

Warren Bennis

Exemplary leaders seem to expect success; they always anticipate positive outcomes. The glass for them is not simply full but brimming.

Warren Bennis

A good leader must be tough enough to win a fight, but not tough enough to kick a man when he is down.

Warren Bennis and E.H. Schein, American management consultants and writers

Lead, follow, or get out of the way.

George Patton (1885–1945), American WWII army general

All of leadership is an Act. It's an act called conveying the Brand Promise via demonstrated High Conviction in pursuit of Great Purpose.

Tom Peters, American management consultant

Leadership is not a solo act; it's a team performance.

James Kouzes and Barry Posner, American management consultants and authors of *Leadership Challenge* and *A Leader's Legacy*

Charisma is, above all, a relationship, a mutual mingling of the inner selves of leader and follower.

Professor Charles Lindholm, American, Boston University anthropologist and author of *Charisma*

Political leaders were usually a combination of darkness and light. The darkness of insecurity, depression, family disorder. In great leaders, the light overcomes the darkness.

Bill Clinton, former American president

I believe in a benevolent dictatorship—as long as I am the benevolent dictator.

Sir Richard Branson, British businessman and founder of the Virgin Group

Be like jockey Willie Shoemaker. He's the best in the business because he has the lightest touch on the reins. They say the horse never knows he's there—unless he's needed.

Harvey Mackay, American, founder and CEO of the Mackay Envelope Company

The final test of a leader is that he leaves behind him in other men the conviction and the will to carry on.

Walter Lippmann (1889–1974), American journalist

Do we want a prime minister who looks like a dentist?

Dame Edna Everage (a character played by Australian comedian Barry Humphries), from 2007 show *Back with a Vengeance* about Australian prime minister John Howard

Leadership is being able to encourage people to follow you to a place that is better than where they are.

Michael Hawker, Australian, managing director and chief executive of insurance company IAG

Management is doing things right; leadership is doing the right things.

Peter Drucker (1909–2005), American-Austrian management academic and writer

Leadership is not rank, privileges, title or money. It is responsibility.

Peter Drucker

I was the first one to talk about leadership 50 years ago, but there is too much talk, too much emphasis on it today and not enough on effectiveness.

Peter Drucker

Leadership is personal. It is unlikely that you will be able to inspire, arouse, excite, or motivate people unless you can show them who you are, what you stand for, and what you can and cannot do.

Rob Goffee and Gareth Jones, authors of *Why Should Anyone Be Led by You? What It Takes to Be an Authentic Leader*

The leader has to have a moral agenda. If the leader is only saying we want to be the biggest or the most profitable company in the world, forget it.

Dame Anita Roddick (1942–2007), British businesswoman and founder of The Body Shop

The first responsibility of a leader is to define reality. The last is to say thank you. In between the two, the leader must become a servant and debtor.

Max DePree, American writer and businessman and author of *Leadership is an Art* and *Leadership Jazz*

Lies, damned lies and statistics

There are three kinds of lies: lies, damned lies and statistics.

Benjamin Disraeli (1804–1881), British prime minister (quote often wrongly attributed to Mark Twain)

They were consistently good at levitating the numbers.

John Olson, American investment analyst, about failed American utility company, Enron, and their financial statements

I did not enter the Labour Party forty-seven years ago to have our manifesto written by Dr Mori, Dr Gallup and Mr Harris.

Tony Benn, former British Labour minister about political pollsters

While statistics are interesting, they are all in the past.

Vince Lombardi (1913–1970), American football coach

He uses statistics as a drunken man uses lamp posts—for support rather than illumination.

Andrew Lang (1844–1912), Scottish writer

It is better to be vaguely right than precisely wrong.

Wildon Carr (1857–1931), British philosopher

Get your facts first then you can distort them as you please.

Mark Twain (1835–1910), American writer

If you want a simple model for predicting the unemployment rate in the United States over the next few years, here it is: It will be what Greenspan wants it to be, plus or minus a random error reflecting the fact that he is not quite God.

Paul Klugman, American, *New York Times* columnist about economist and former chairman of the board of governors of the Federal Reserve, Alan Greenspan

It has been my experience that competency in mathematics, both in numerical manipulations and in understanding its conceptual foundations, enhances a person's ability to handle the more ambiguous and qualitative relationships that dominate our day-to-day financial decision-making.

Alan Greenspan, American economist and former chairman of the board of governors of the Federal Reserve

To succeed, you will soon learn, as I did, the importance of a solid foundation in the basics of education—literacy, both verbal and numerical, and communication skills.

Alan Greenspan

Just because your ratings are bigger doesn't mean you're better.

Ted Turner, American businessman and founder of CNN

Management

> You can no longer manage a workforce. You manage individuals.
>
> Peter Drucker (1909–2005), American-Austrian management academic and writer

Checking the results of a decision against its expectations shows executives what their strengths are, where they need to improve, and where they lack knowledge or information.

Peter Drucker

I hope that when the epitaphs are being written, they will say that this was one of the first companies to try to change the language and the behaviour of business, that brought a social engagement to everything it did, and shouted this from the rooftops.

Dame Anita Roddick (1942–2007), British businesswoman and founder of The Body Shop

It is amazing what you can accomplish if you do not care who gets the credit.

Harry S. Truman (1884–1972), American president

What separates winners from losers is not the brilliance of the strategic plan. It is the way a company organises and motivates its people. In 1976, this was a very strange and very wild idea.

Tom Peters, American management consultant

Whenever there is a hard job to be done I assign it to a lazy man; he is sure to find an easy way of doing it.

Walter Chrysler (1875–1940), American, founder of the Chrysler Corporation (one of the US Big Three auto manufacturers until 1998)

If we aren't careful, we can wind up treating people at work like dogs: continually rewarding those who heap unthinking, unconditional admiration upon us. What behavior do we get in return? A virulent case of the suck-ups.

Marshall Goldsmith, American, author of *What Got You Here Won't Get You There*

The problem is not that there are problems. The problem is expecting otherwise and thinking that having problems is a problem.

Theodore Rubin, American psychiatrist

The surest way for an executive to kill himself is to refuse to learn how and when and to whom to delegate.

James C. Penney (1875–1971), American, founder of the J.C. Penney stores

Never tell people how to do things. Tell them what to do and they will surprise you with their ingenuity.

George S. Patton (1885–1945), American military leader in World War II

A corporation is a living organism; it has to continue to shed its skin. Methods have to change. Focus has to change. Values have to change. The sum total of those changes is transformation.

Andrew Grove, American-Hungarian business executive and co-founder of Intel

Meetings are a great trap. Soon you find yourself trying to get agreement and then the people who disagree come to think they have a right to be persuaded. However, they are indispensable when you don't want to do anything.

John Kenneth Galbraith (1908–2006), American-Canadian economist

If I had to sum up in one word what makes a good manager, I'd say decisiveness. You can use the fanciest computers to gather the numbers, but in the end you have to set a timetable and act.

Lee Iacocca, American business executive

Removing people will always be the hardest decision a leader faces. Anyone who 'enjoys doing it' shouldn't be on the payroll, and neither should anyone who 'can't do it'.

Jack Welch, American, former General Electric CEO

Giving people self-confidence is by far the most important thing that I can do. Because then they will act.

Jack Welch

An overburdened, overstretched executive is the best executive, because he or she doesn't have the time to meddle, to deal in trivia, to bother people.

Jack Welch

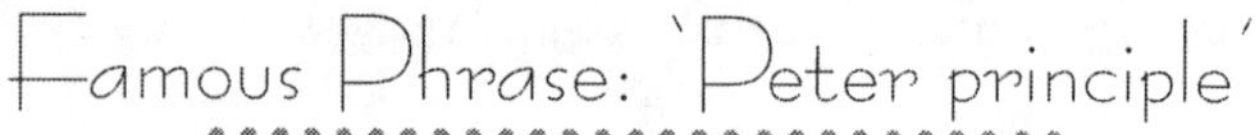

Famous Phrase: 'Peter principle'

In a hierarchy every employee tends to rise to his level of incompetence.

Laurence J. Peter (1919–1990), Canadian academic

Manners and persuasion

This is an age of social autism, in which people just can't see the value of imagining their impact on others, and in which responsibility is always conveniently laid at other people's doors.

Lynne Truss, English writer

Manners are the lubricating oil of an organisation.

Peter Drucker (1909–2005), American-Austrian management academic and writer

Good breeding consists of concealing how much we think of ourselves and how little we think of the other person.

Mark Twain (1835–1910), American writer

When will conventional good manners become attractive? When will ladies of fashion exhibit their shoulders a little less and their affability and wit a little more?

Honore de Balzac (1799–1850), French writer

Those who have mastered etiquette, who are entirely, impeccably right, would seem to arrive at a point of exquisite dullness.

Dorothy Parker (1893–1967), American writer

He is tremendously persuasive. He can convince all sorts of people, from Boy George to city investors, that it might be a good idea to tag along.

Don Cruikshank, Virgin managing director about Sir Richard Branson

You go into his office wanting to kill him and you come out thinking that maybe he's right after all.

Michael Smith, Lesotho Diamond Corporation shareholder, about convicted Australian fraudster Alan Bond

The tendency to conformity in our society is so strong that reasonably intelligent and well-meaning young people are willing to call white, black.

Solomon Asch (1907–1996), American-Polish psychologist, about 1950s research on people's desire to conform

Manners are a sensitive awareness of the feelings of others. If you have that awareness, you have good manners, no matter what fork you use.

Emily Post (1873–1960), American etiquette writer

Laughter ... the most civilised music in the world.

Peter Ustinov (1921–2004), Brtish actor

At a dinner party one should eat wisely but not too well, and talk well but not too wisely.

Somerset Maugham (1874–1965), British writer

Bedside manners are no substitute for the right diagnosis.

Alfred Sloan Jr (1875–1966), American businessman and chairman of General Motors

Savages, we call them, because their manners differ from ours.

Benjamin Franklin (1706–1790), American politician and 'founding father' about native North Americans with whom Franklin had extensive contact and respect

To succeed in the world it is not enough to be stupid, you must also be well-mannered.

Voltaire (1694–1778), French philosopher and writer

Manners are especially the need of the plain. The pretty can get away with anything.

Evelyn Waugh (1903–1966), British novelist

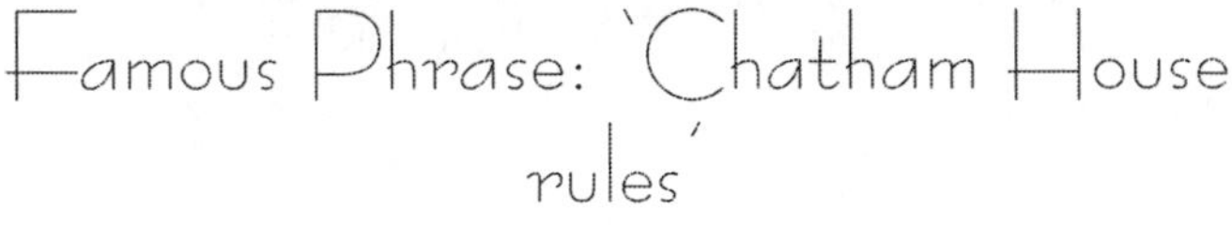

When a meeting, or part thereof, is held under the Chatham House Rule, participants are free to use the information received, but neither the identity nor the affiliation of the speaker(s), nor that of any other participant, may be revealed.

From Chatham House, a British NGO which analyses international affairs

Media

Good journalism helps define the character of societies. Its absence leads to societies that are more mediocre in every way.

Eric Beecher, Australian media proprietor and former newspaper editor

I do not pretend to gaze into the crystal ball and foresee all that will happen in the future. That divine right or gift is given only to the editors of newspapers.

Ben Chifley (1885–1951), Australian Labor prime minister

Many people think that for a journal to be popular it must follow public opinion. This is a grand mistake. A journal that waits for public opinion to be formed before it expresses its own opinion will infallibly incur, not the support, but the contempt of the public and deservedly so.

David Syme (1827–1908), Australian newspaper proprietor

Blood sport is brought to its ultimate refinement in the gossip columns.

Sir Bernard Ingham, English, press secretary of former British prime minister, Margaret Thatcher

The Telegraph is being run like a cocktail party in a banana republic.

Simon Heffer, British journalist about newspaper proprietor, Conrad Black's management style

All newspapers are run to make profits. Full stop. I don't run anything for respectability. The moment I do, I hope someone will come and fire me and get me out of the place—because that's not what newspapers are meant to be about.

Rupert Murdoch, Australian-American businessman

We've got journalism in the blood. I've tried very hard to imbue my own children with the same thing. It carries special responsibilities.

Rupert Murdoch

I can't concede this difference between quality papers and mass circulation popular papers.

Rupert Murdoch

I ran the paper purely for propaganda and with no other purpose.

Lord Beaverbrook (1879–1964), British newspaper proprietor

I'm very worried that Dow Jones' unique journalistic values will long-term strongly suffer after the proposed sale.

Dieter von Holtbrink, former Dow Jones employee about then probable sale of the company to Rupert Murdoch's News Corporation

No self-respecting fish would be wrapped in a Murdoch newspaper.

Mike Royko (1932–1997), American journalist who resigned from the *Chicago Sun–Times* when Murdoch bought the paper

When you see yourself quoted in print and you're sorry you said it, it suddenly becomes a misquotation.

Laurence J. Peter (1919–1990), Canadian academic

I read the newspapers avidly. It is my one form of continuous fiction.

Aneurin Bevan (1897–1960), British Labour politician

It seems to me elementary that if you've got the story that's going to dominate history you might as well go right to the president.

Ben Bradlee, American journalist and editor of *Washington Post* during the Watergate crisis, which started off as an office break-in but became the story that brought down a president

Maybe not all of you are familiar with what it takes to make a great newspaper. It takes a great owner. Period.

Ben Bradlee at the funeral of *Washington Post* owner, Katherine Graham

When you're young, you look at television and think, there's a conspiracy. The networks have conspired to dumb us down. But when you get a little older, you realise that's not true. The networks are in business to give people exactly what they want. That's a far more depressing thought. Conspiracy is optimistic!

Steve Jobs, American businessman and founder of Apple Computers

But when reporters say to me I'm only doing this because it's my job … that's the same abdication of moral responsibility at the thin end of the wedge that in its most extreme and horrific version ends up with others being prepared to stand as a concentration camp guard.

Ken Livingstone, British Labour politician and Mayor of London

No-one's interested in f***ing flood control—go for the interview with Noah.

Don Hewitt, veteran American *60 Minutes* journalist

The one function that TV news performs very well is that when there is no news we give it to you with the same emphasis as if there were.

David Brinkley (1920–2003), American broadcaster

A senior politician is only ever a soundbite away from destruction.

David Mellor, British Conservative politician

One of the great self-inflicted wounds of Britain in the 1980s was to allow so many of its newspapers to fall into the hands of foreign companies.

David Mellor

I believe that the person concerned would not be capable of reporting accurately a minute's silence.

Jim Killen (1925–2007), Australian conservative politician

The camera cannot lie. But it can be an accessory to untruth.

Harold Evans, American-British journalist and editor

In the old days you adjourned Parliament and got away quickly. Now we are subject to press conferences and television interviews and treated broadly as dishonest witnesses in criminal cases.

Harold Macmillan (1894–1986), British prime minister

A terminal blight has hit the TV industry nipping fun in the bud and stunting our growth. This blight is management—the dreaded four Ms: male, middle class, middle-aged and mediocre.

Janet Street-Porter, British broadcaster and journalist

Never pick a fight with people who buy ink by the barrel.

Mark Twain (1835–1910), American writer (frequently attributed to Bill Clinton)

We don't just have egg on our face. We have omelette all over our suits.

Tom Brokaw, American journalist about televison networks' premature calls about the 2000 American presidential election results

Our liberty depends on freedom of the press, and that cannot be limited without being lost.

Thomas Jefferson (1743–1826), American president

Television in the main is being used to distract, delude, amuse and insulate us.

Edward R. Murrow (1880–1965), American journalist

This is the crack cocaine of journalism.

James Carville, American political consultant most widely known for his advice to Bill Clinton during 1992 presidential campaign—about the 'bimbo eruptions' of that campaign

I am going to say something that few people in public life will say, but most know is absolutely true: a vast aspect of our jobs today—outside of the really major decisions, as big as anything else—is coping with the media, its sheer scale, weight and constant hyperactivity. At points, it literally overwhelms.

Tony Blair, former British Labour prime minister, in one of his last speeches as PM

Not to have a proper press operation nowadays is like asking a batsman to face bodyline bowling without pads or headgear.

Tony Blair

The new media age lowers barriers to entry. It unleashes vast energy but also potentially undermines standards of reliability, accountability, trust and accuracy.

Michael Ovitz, American businessman

Television brought the brutality of war into the comfort of the living room. Vietnam was lost in the living rooms of America—not the battlefields of Vietnam.

Marshall McLuhan (1911–1980), Canadian academic

In the early days of television, when there were only half a dozen channels at most, significant, well-written dramas on a cathode ray tube could still make us feel like members of an attentive congregation, alone at home as we might be.

Kurt Vonnegut (1922–2007), American writer

The business press tends to rivet our attention on the Icarus companies—high profile firms either on the way up or the day down.

James C. Collins and Jerry I. Porras, authors of *Built to Last*

Because television can make so much money doing its worst, it often cannot afford to do its best.

Fred Friendly (1915–1998), American television broadcaster and business executive

Motivation

Being the richest man in the cemetery doesn't matter to me … Going to bed at night saying we've done something wonderful … that's what matters to me.

Steve Jobs, American businessman and founder of Apple Computers

People who never get carried away, should be.

Steve Forbes, American magazine publisher

Constantly refine your gene pool ... by promoting your best performers and weeding out your worst.

Jack Welch, American, former General Electric CEO

You can't just reward people with trophies. Reward them in the wallet, too.

Jack Welch

You get paid a lot, but the real payoff is the fun.

Jack Welch

Two things kept me going: Jesus Christ and mascara.

Tammy Faye Messner (previously Bakker) (1942–2007), American evangelist and former wife of convicted televangelist Jim Bakker and recognisable by her excessive use of eye makeup

Without passion, you don't have energy; without energy, you have nothing. Nothing great in the world has been accomplished without passion.

Donald Trump, American businessman

Money was never a big motivation for me, except as a way to keep score. The real excitement is playing the game.

Donald Trump

Sometimes your best investments are the ones you don't make.

Donald Trump

You grab a paper and there is a rush, there is adrenalin. Good God—look what we said today! It's more than you can get out of baked beans.

Tony O'Reilly, Irish newspaper owner

Most people get into bands for three very simple rock and roll reasons: to get laid, to get fame, and to get rich.

Bob Geldof, Irish musician and activist

This is not a time for soundbites. We've left them at home. I feel the hand of history upon our shoulders. I'm here to try.

Tony Blair, former British Labour prime minister, about the final stage of Northern Irish negotiations, 1998

You can do anything if you have enthusiasm. Enthusiasm is the yeast that makes your hopes rise to the stars. With it, there is accomplishment. Without it there are only alibis.

Henry Ford (1863–1947), American, founder of the Ford Motor Company

I just love it when people say I can't do it, there's nothing that makes me feel better because all my life, people have said that I wasn't going to make it.

Ted Turner, American businessman and founder of CNN

There are two times in a man's life when he should not speculate: when he can't afford it and when he can.

Mark Twain (1835–1910), American writer

Reward excellent failures. Punish mediocre success.

Phil Daniels, Australian businessman

Benefits should be granted little by little so that they may be better enjoyed.

Niccolo Machiavelli (1469–1527), Italian political philosopher

Why not go out on a limb? That's where the fruit is.

Will Rogers (1879–1935), American actor and writer

I love trying to create new businesses, and I like trying to take on the big established companies.

Sir Richard Branson, British businessman and founder of the Virgin Group

When you've parked the second car in the garage, and installed the hot tub, and skied in Colorado, and wind-surfed in the Caribbean, when you've had your first love affair and your second and your third, the question will remain, where does the dream end for me?

Sir Richard Branson

A business has to be involving, it has to be fun, and it has to exercise your creative instincts.

Sir Richard Branson

If the question is, how would I wish to be remembered, I guess I'd have to say, not as somebody who spent his life in a balloon.

Sir Richard Branson

Vote for the man who promises least; he'll be the least disappointing.

Bernard Baruch (1870–1965), American presidential adviser and investor

British electors will never vote for a man who doesn't wear a hat.

Lord Beaverbrook (1879–1964) British newspaper proprietor, advice to a political aspirant

When I joined the Labor Party it was made up of the cream of the working class. When I left it was made up of the dregs of the middle class.

Kim Beazley Sr (1917–2007), Australian former federal Labor minister (attributed)

Greed is all right ... Greed is healthy. You can be greedy and still feel good about yourself.

Ivan Boesky, American investor imprisoned in 1987 for insider trading

Bill Hewlett and Dave Packard's ultimate creation wasn't the audio oscilloscope or the pocket calculator. It was the Hewlett-Packard Company and the HP Way.

James C. Collins and Jerry I. Porras, American management academics and authors of *Built to Last*, about the company's management style

An incentive is simply a means of urging people to do more of a good thing and less of a bad thing.

Steven D. Levitt and Stephen J. Dubner, American authors of *Freakonomics*

There are three basic flavors of incentive: economic, social and moral.

Steven D. Levitt and Stephen J. Dubner

The typical economist believes the world has not yet invented a problem that he cannot fix if given a free hand to design the proper incentive scheme.

Steven D. Levitt and Stephen J. Dubner

In all life one should comfort the afflicted, but verily, also, one should afflict the comfortable, and especially when they are comfortably, contentedly, even happily wrong.

John Kenneth Galbraith (1908–2006), American-Canadian economist

There is something wonderful in seeing a wrong-headed majority assailed by truth.

John Kenneth Galbraith

Past, present and future

When I was younger, we had Virgin Nightclubs. Now we have Virgin Health Clubs. I guess Virgin Funerals are inevitable.

Sir Richard Branson, British businessman and founder of the Virgin Group

What then is, generally speaking, the truth of history? A fable agreed upon.

Napoleon I (1769–1821), French military leader and emperor

What is not recorded is not remembered.

Benazir Bhutto, former Pakistani prime minister

It's *déjà vu* all over again.

Yogi Berra, American, former baseball player

If we know what the future is, we aren't looking far enough ahead.

Sir Tim Berners-Lee, English, co-inventor of the World Wide Web

We must reinvent a future free of blinders so that we can choose from real options.

David Suzuki, Canadian scientist and environmental activist

I do not know which makes a man more conservative—to know nothing but the present, or nothing but the past.

John Maynard Keynes (1883–1946), British economist

The wogs and reffos of yesterday are the TV chefs, sporting heroes and business and political success stories of today.

Peter Garrett, Australian federal Labor politician and former Midnight Oil frontman about Australian post-war migration

I told them that my grandfather had died in the Great Crash of 1929—a stockbroker jumped out of a window and crushed him and his pushcart down below.

Mario Cuomo, American Democrat politician and former New York City mayor

The factory of the future will have only two employees, a man and a dog. The man will be there to feed the dog. The dog will be there to keep the man from touching the equipment.

Warren Bennis, American management writer and consultant

Two trends will cycle high in our culture: cocooning, our desire to shelter ourselves from the harsh realities of our world, and fantasy adventure, our hunger for the new and unconventional.

Faith Popcorn, American futurist

The best way to predict the future is to invent it.

Alan Kay, American IT scientist and businessman

Trying to predict the future is like trying to drive down a country road at night with no lights while looking out the back window.

Peter Drucker (1909–2005), American-Austrian management academic and writer

The best time to fix the roof is when the sun is shining.

John F. Kennedy (1917–1963), American Democrat president

The corporation as we know it, which is now 120 years old, is not likely to survive the next 25 years. Legally and financially yes, but not structurally and economically.

Peter Drucker

At least 80 per cent of white-collar jobs, as we know them today, will either disappear entirely or be reconfigured beyond recognition in just 15 years.

Tom Peters, American management consultant

The data superhighway is the most important marketplace of the 21st century.

Al Gore, former American Democrat vice president

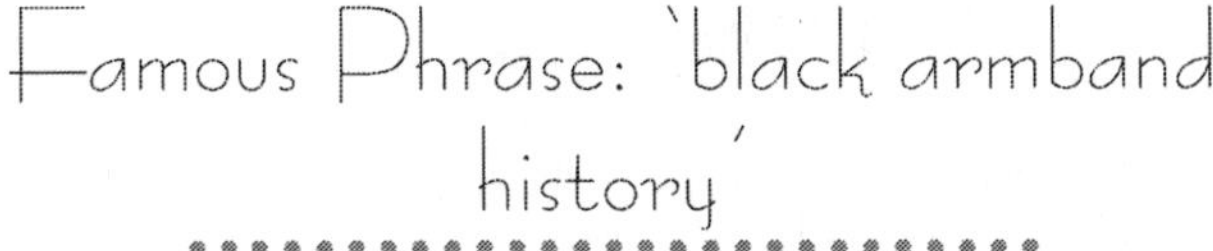

Famous Phrase: 'black armband history'

The 'black armband' view of our history reflects a belief that most Australian history since 1788 has been little more than a disgraceful story of imperialism, exploitation, racism, sexism and other forms of discrimination. I take a very different view. I believe that the balance sheet of our history is one of heroic achievement and that we have achieved much more as a nation of which we can be proud of than which we should be ashamed.

John Howard, Australian Prime Minister

Paul Keating

Former Australian Labor prime minister Paul Keating is well known for his colourful language.

Politics has always been an ideas market. When you run the ideas, you run the market.

The thing about poor old Costello is he is all tip and no iceberg. He can throw a punch across the parliament but the bloke he should be throwing a punch to is Howard, but of course he doesn't have the ticker for it.

Peter Costello has been the deputy leader of Australia's Liberal Party since 1994 and Treasurer of Australia since 1996

The old coconut is still there Araldited to the seat. The treasurer works on the smart quips but when it comes to staring down the prime minister in his office he always leaves disappointed.

About the John Howard/Peter Costello leadership rivalry which Costello has repeatedly retreated from

Prime ministers have got Araldite glue on their pants, most of them, and you either put the sword through them or you let the public do it.

If this government cannot get manufacturing going again and keep moderate wage outcomes and a sensible economic policy, then Australia is basically done for, we end up being a third-rate economy ... Then you are gone. You are a banana republic.

Does a soufflé rise twice?

In 1989 about Liberal party

The most important thing about that, is that this is a recession that Australia had to have.

About the 1991–92 Australian recession

When we put our federation together, there were no Washingtons around, no soldier statesmen, no people like Jefferson talking about blood being the fertiliser of the democracy. It was put together by lawyers and businessmen—mostly old forelock tuggers—who set us up as a British satellite.

Even as it walked out on you and joined the common market, you were still looking for your MBEs and your knighthoods, and all the rest of the regalia that comes with it. You would take Australia right back down the time tunnel to the cultural cringe where you have always come from.

We will not adopt the fantastic hypocrisy of modern conservatism which preaches the values of families and communities, while conducting a direct assault on them through reduced wages and conditions and job security.

I'm watching you and you're a low flyer.

If you want to impress the visitors, of course, you come to Sydney.

Sydney is the only place to live in Australia—the rest is camping out.

The public has a right to look at the harbour without a sea of plastic, of clanking aluminium masts and Tupperware boats as far as the eye can see.

I've saved a bit of the bush in my time, like the Daintree. But on the whole I'm happy to leave all that to sandal-wearing, muesli-eating types like Bob Carr.

I walk on that stage, some performances might be better than others, but they will all be up there trying to stream the economics and politics together. Out there on the stage doing the Placido Domingo.

It was we who did the dispossessing. We took the traditional lands and smashed the traditional way of life. We brought the diseases, the alcohol. We committed the murders. We took the children from their mothers. We practised discrimination and exclusion. It was our ignorance and our prejudice. And our failure to imagine these things being done to us.

From Keating's 1992 Redfern speech. Redfern is an important area to the Aboriginal community.

The Labor Party is not going to profit from having these proven unsuccessful people around who are frightened of their own shadow and won't get out of bed in the morning unless they've had a focus group report to tell them which side of bed to get out.

I was told I did not learn respect at school. I learnt one thing: I learnt about self-respect and self-regard for Australia—not about some cultural cringe to a country which decided not to defend the Malaysian peninsula, not to worry about Singapore and not to give us our troops back to keep ourselves free from Japanese domination.

He's a really charming, old-fashioned, good Catholic boy.

Joan Kirner, Australian former Victorian Labor premier about Keating

People and teamwork

No matter how good or successful you are or how clever or crafty, your business and its future are in the hands of the people you hire.

Akio Morita (1921–1999), Japanese, co-founder and former CEO of Sony

Getting the right people in the right jobs is a lot more important than developing a strategy.

Jack Welch, American, former General Electric CEO

Employees may be our greatest liability, but people are our greatest opportunity.

Peter Drucker (1909–2005), American-Austrian management academic and writer

Outstanding leaders go out of their way to boost the self-esteem of their personnel. If people believe in themselves, it's amazing what they can accomplish.

Sam Walton (1918–1992), American, Wal-Mart founder

Nothing else can quite substitute for a few well-chosen, well-timed, sincere words of praise. They're absolutely free—and worth a fortune.

Sam Walton

You can't treat people like an expense item.

Andrew Grove, American-Hungarian business executive and co-founder of Intel

The workplace should primarily be an incubator for the human spirit.

Dame Anita Roddick (1942–2007), British businesswoman and founder of The Body Shop

Michael, if you can't pass, you can't play.

Dean Smith, American basketball coach, to Michael Jordan in his first year with a university team

The people who are doing the work are the moving force behind the Macintosh. My job is to create a space for them, to clear out the rest of the organisation and keep it at bay.

Steve Jobs, American businessman and founder of Apple Computers

People are definitely a company's greatest asset. It doesn't make any difference whether the product is cars or cosmetics. A company is only as good as the people it keeps.

Mary Kay Ash (1918–2001), American, founder and former CEO of Mary Kay Cosmetics

We are all different. A good manager will recognise those differences and treat each person as an individual.

Mary Kay Ash

Teamwork requires open, two-way communication and trust.

John Chambers, American, Cisco Systems chairman and CEO

Now, if your boss is a sadist, then you have a big problem. In that case, fire your boss and get a new job.

Donald Trump, American businessman

If you have a happy group of people working for you, you can pretty well do anything.

Sir Richard Branson, British businessman and founder of the Virgin Group

A team will perform well only if peak performance is elicited from the individuals in it.

Andrew Grove, American-Hungarian business executive and co-founder of Intel

Working collectively and collaboratively is the difference between mediocrity by yourself ... or success as a team. You have to share the pain ... and the responsibility ... and if you do then you will also share in the rewards.

Michael Bloomberg, American businessman and New York City mayor

First, make yourself a reputation for being a creative genius. Second, surround yourself with partners who are better than you are. Third, leave them to go get on with it.

David Ogilvy (1911–1999), American-English advertising executive

Politics and government

The thing about the job is its utter relentlessness. It never leaves you. Never. It is emotionally, physically and mentally draining.

Tony Blair, former British Labour prime minister

The hardest thing about leadership is learning to ignore the loudest voices ... both support and opposition.

Tony Blair

Loyalty is a fine quality, but in excess it fills political graveyards.

Neil Kinnock, former British Labour politician

I think it is just stupid economics for a government to approach economic management from a strand of thinking regarding unions as enemies.

Bob Hawke, former Australian Labor prime minister

If the policy isn't hurting, it isn't working.

John Major, former British Conservative prime minister

If you want to succeed in politics, you must keep your conscience well under control.

David Lloyd George (1863–1945), British Liberal politician

There are no problems we cannot solve together, and very few we can solve by ourselves.

Lyndon Baines Johnson (1908–1973), American president

When your opponent is drowning, throw the son of a bitch an anvil.

James Carville, American political consultant to candidates including Bill Clinton in 1992

Once the toothpaste is out of the tube, it is awfully hard to get it back in.

H.R. Haldeman (1929–1993), aide to President Richard Nixon during the Watergate crisis

I don't know whether it's the finest public housing in America or the crown jewel of the federal prison system.

Bill Clinton, former American president, on life in the White House

I knew that he who wields the knife never wears the crown.

Michael Heseltine, British Conservative politician, about the aftermath of his role in the overthrow of Margaret Thatcher as prime minister in 1990

All politics is local.

Thomas 'Tip' O'Neill (1912–1994), American Democrat politician

All politics, however, are based on the indifference of the majority.

James Reston (1909–1995), American journalist

Please assure me that you are all Republicans!

Ronald Reagan (1911–2004), American president to emergency medical staff following the 1981 assassination attempt

You want a friend in Washington? Get a dog.

Harry S. Truman (1884–1972), American president

Don't worry, it's a slam dunk.

George Tenet, former head of American intelligence agency, CIA, who used this phrase about evidence of 'weapons of mass destruction' in Saddam Hussein's Iraq prior to the 2003 invasion

The House of Lords is like a glass of champagne that has stood for five days.

Clement Attlee (1883–1967), British prime minister

When you focus on solving problems instead of scoring political points, and emphasise common sense over ideology, you'd be surprised what can be accomplished.

Barack Obama, American Democrat senator and 2008 presidential candidate

A body of five hundred men chosen at random from amongst the unemployed.

David Lloyd George (1863–1945), British Liberal politician about the House of Lords

Politics is a marathon not a sprint.

Ken Livingstone, British Labour politician and Mayor of London

Any woman who understands the problems of running a home will be nearer to understanding the problems of running a country.

Margaret Thatcher, former British prime minister

Balancing the budget is like going to heaven. Everybody wants to do it, but nobody wants to do what you have to do to get there.

Phil Gramm, American Republican politician

I believe there is something out there watching over us. Unfortunately, it is the government.

Woody Allen, American filmmaker, actor and comedian

Without any inhibitions of any kind, I make it quite clear that Australia looks to America, free of any pangs as to our traditional links or kinship with the United Kingdom.

John Curtin (1885–1945), Australian Labor prime minister during World War II when the conflict in South East Asia threatened Australia and the UK focus was on Europe

I always cheer up immensely if an attack is particularly wounding because I think, well, if they attack one personally, it means they have not a single political argument left.

Margaret Thatcher, former British prime minister

Ask me my three main priorities for government, and I tell you: education, education and education.

Tony Blair, former British Labour prime minister

Politics is not the art of the possible. It consists of choosing between the disastrous and the unpalatable.

John Kenneth Galbraith (1908–2006), American-Canadian economist to President John Kennedy

The good of man must be the objective of the science of politics.

Aristotle (384–322 BC), Greek philosopher

Politics is the art of looking for trouble, finding it everywhere, diagnosing it incorrectly and applying the wrong remedies.

Groucho Marx (1890–1977), American comedian and actor

Politics is the art of the possible.

Prince Otto von Bismarck (1815–1898), German statesman in 1867

Just remember that political courage is not political suicide.

Arnold Schwarzenegger, American-Austrian Republican Governor of California, former actor and bodybuilder

Politics is the art of preventing people from taking part in affairs which properly concern them.

Pal Valey (1871–1945), French writer

How can you govern a country which has 246 varieties of cheese?

Charles de Gaulle (1890–1970), French president

No easy problems ever come to the president of the United States. If they are easy to solve, someone else has solved them.

Dwight Eisenhower (1890–1969), American president

NSW politics is a blood sport in which people are torn down but fortunately I've been able to survive.

Neville Wran, Australian former NSW Labor premier

What is politics but persuading the public to vote for this and support that and endure these for the promise of those?

Gilbert Highet (1906–1978), Scottish-American writer

[The Soviet government] is the most realistic regime in the world—no ideals.

Golda Meir (1898–1978), Prime Minister of Israel

The single most exciting thing you encounter in government is competence, because it's so rare.

Daniel P. Moynihan (1927–2003), American Senator and sociologist

For a country to have a great writer is like having a second government. That is why no regime has ever loved great writers, only minor ones.

Alexander Solzhenitsyn, Russian novelist, dramatist and historian

Our constitution works. Our great republic is a government of laws, not of men.

Gerald R. Ford (1913–2006), American president

Read my lips: no new taxes.

George Bush Sr, former American president, one of modern politics' most famous broken promises

I'm so overexposed, I'm making Paris Hilton look like a recluse.

Barack Obama, American Democrat senator and 2008 presidential candidate

You're an analogue politician in a digital age.

David Cameron, former British Conservative opposition leader, about Gordon Brown when he was Chancellor of the Exchequer

If Hillary Rodham Clinton is the nurturer-warrior and Barack Obama the college idealist and John McCain the tough but irreverent flyboy, then Mr Giuliani is the father, the talk-tough-on-terror, I'm-comfortable-wielding-authority guy.

Michael Powell, *New York Times* journalist, about 2008 American presidential candidates

Peter Mandelson is someone who can skulk in broad daylight.

Simon Hoggart, British journalist, about a British Labour politician who was forced to resign twice from Tony Blair's cabinet

Ronald Reagan, the president who never told bad news to the American people.

Garrison Keillor, American writer, musician and radio personality

You are honoured by your friends, distinguished by your enemies. I have been very distinguished.

Herbert Hoover (1895–1972), American president

New York City Mayor Michael Bloomberg has quit the Republican Party … and has become an Independent. Bloomberg says he has no plans to be president. Now don't confuse that with President Bush, who has no plans as president.

Jay Leno, American talkshow host

Lyndon B. Johnson always thought that Australia was the next large rectangular state beyond El Paso, and treated it accordingly.

Marshall Green, American ambassador to Australia during 1970s

In Iran, President Ahmadinejad is apparently so unpopular that the parliament has voted to take away his powers and shorten his term. When he heard this, President Bush said, 'That lucky bastard'.

Conan O'Brien, American comedian

I wouldn't vote for Ken Livingstone if he were running for the Mayor of Toytown.

Arthur Scargill, British trade unionist

There are few things more amusing in the world of politics than watching moderate Republicans charging to the right in pursuit of greater glory.

Mario Cuomo, American Democrat politician and former New York City mayor

I have been underestimated for decades. I have done very well that way.

Helmut Kohl, former West German chancellor

A thick skin is a gift from God.

Konrad Adenauer (1876–1967), West German chancellor

All the security around the American president is just to make sure the man who shoots him gets caught.

Norman Mailer (1923–2007), American writer

A politician was a person with whose politics you did not agree. When you did agree, he was a statesman.

David Lloyd George (1863–1945), British Liberal politician

Being an MP feeds your vanity and starves your self-respect.

Matthew Parris, British writer and former Conservative politician

A statesman is a politician who places himself at the service of the nation. A politician is a statesman who places the nation at his service.

Georges Pompidou (1911–1974), French president

The further you got from Britain, the more admired you found she was.

James Callaghan (1912–2005), British Labour prime minister about Margaret Thatcher

The Australian Labor Party does not even call itself a socialist party. Actually it is a liberal-bourgeois party, while the so-called Liberals in Australia are really Conservatives.

Vladimir Lenin (1870–1924), Russian revolutionary and first leader of the Soviet Union in 1913

Healey's first law of politics: when you're in a hole, stop digging.

Dennis Healey, former British Labour minister

It's not a lot different than being an actor, except I get to write the script.

Ronald Reagan (1911–2004), American president, in answer to a question from Bob Hope about what is was like being president

Intelligence reports say he, Castro, is very worried about me. I'm very worried that we can't come up with something to justify his worrying.

Ronald Reagan, from *The Reagan Diaries*

Guns will make us powerful; butter will only make us fat.

Hermann Goering (1893–1946), German military leader during Hitler's Third Reich

Unlimited power is apt to corrupt the minds of those who possess it.

William Pitt (1708–1778), British prime minister

Sometimes the only way you conquer the pull of power is to set it down.

Tony Blair, former British Labour prime minister

No one can terrorise a whole nation, unless we are all his accomplices.

Ed Murrow (1908–1965), American journalist about Joseph McCarthy

I'm President of the United States and I'm not going to eat any more broccoli!

George Bush Sr, former American president

So long as men worship the Caesars and Napoloeons, Caesars and Napoleons will duly arise and make them miserable.

Aldous Huxley (1894–1963), British writer

Office tends to confer a dreadful plausibility on even the most negligible of those who hold it.

Mark Lawson, British journalist

Every Communist must grasp the truth, 'Political power grows out of the barrel of a gun'.

Mao Zedong (1893–1976), first leader of Communist China

It is better to die on your feet than to live on your knees.

Dolores Ibarruri (1895–1989), Spanish Communist leader, during Spanish Civil War in 1936

Take all your dukes and marquesses and earls and viscounts, pack them into one chamber, call it the House of Lords to satisfy their pride and then strip it of all political power. It's a solution so perfectly elegant and preposterous that only the British could have managed it.

Charles Krauthammer, Canadian-American columnist and commentator

Public service

And thus Bureaucracy, the giant power wielded by pigmies, came into the world.

Honore de Balzac (1799–1850), French writer

Guidelines for bureaucrats: (1) When in charge, ponder. (2) When in trouble, delegate. (3) When in doubt, mumble.

James H. Boren, American bureaucrat

Bureaucracy defends the status quo long past the time when the quo has lost its status.

Laurence J. Peter (1919–1990), Canadian academic

From 10 to 1 / There's nothing done / From 2 to 3 / We begin to see / That from 3 to 4 / They'll be nothing more!

Sir Edmund Barton (1849–1920), Australian, about the NSW public service when he was a state minister

The president is not the action officer.

George Tenet, former head of America's intelligence agency, about the bureaucracy's rigid chain of command

The Pentagon, that immense monument to modern man's subservience to the desk.

Lord Franks (1905–1992), British administrator

'Under consideration' means we've lost the file. 'Under active consideration' means we're trying to find it.

Sir Humphry Appleby, from the 'Yes Minister' television series

If you want to describe a proposal in a way that guarantees that a minister will reject it, describe it as courageous.

Sir Humphry Appleby

The Civil Service is a bit like a Rolls Royce—you know it's the best machine in the world, but you're not quite sure what to do with it.

R.A. ('Rab') Butler (1902–1992), British Conservative politician

The perfect bureaucrat everywhere is the man who manages to make no decisions and escape all responsibility.

Brooks Atkinson (1894–1984), *New York Times* theatre critic

Government machinery has been described as a marvellous labour saving device which enables ten men to do the work of one.

John Maynard Keynes (1883–1946), British economist

Give a civil servant a good case and he'll wreck it with clichés, bad punctuation, double negatives and convoluted apology.

Alan Clark (1928–1999), British Conservative politician

A bureaucracy always tends to become a pedantocracy.

John Stuart Mill (1806–1873), British economist and philosopher

Cabinet minutes are studied in government departments with the reverence generally reserved for sacred texts, and can be triumphantly produced conclusively to settle any arguments.

Gerald Kaufman, former British Labour politician

Government does not solve problems; it subsidises them.

Ronald Reagan, (1911–2004), American president

The nine most terrifying words in the English language are, 'I'm from the government and I'm here to help'.

Ronald Reagan

Freedom is not America's gift to the world; it is the Almighty God's gift to every man and woman in this world.

George W. Bush, American president

Every dictator uses religion as a prop to keep himself in power.

Benazir Bhutto, former Pakistani prime minister

In Papua New Guinea now we have the job of rebuilding some of those values that have almost been lost and partly destroyed by a Western cult known as Christianity.

Michael Somare, Prime Minister of Papua New Guinea, comment from 1973 before independence

Don't like it, to be honest, when politicians make a big thing of their religious beliefs, so I don't make a big thing of it.

Tony Blair, former British Labour prime minister

You've gone from 45 at your first service in 1983 to a congregation of over 14 000! I've got to tell you that I don't think there's any side of Australian politics that could do a branch stack as good as that.

John Howard, Australian prime minister at the opening of new Hillsong Church premises

Brezhnev and I looked directly across the room at a several-times-life-size mural of Christ and Apostles at the Last Supper. Brezhnev said, 'That was the politburo of those days.'

Richard Nixon (1913–1994), American president

It is a serious moral matter and Catholic politicians who vote for this legislation must realise that their voting has consequences for their place in the life of the church.

George Pell, Australian cardinal, about Australia's NSW parliament's legislation on stem cell research

I think Cardinal Pell has three options: he can apologise, he can run for Parliament or he can invite further comparisons with that serial boofhead Sheik Al Hilali.

Nathan Rees, Australian NSW state Labor politician, in response to Cardinal Pell commenting on political issues. Sheik Hilali was the controversial mufti of Lakemba Mosque in Sydney from 1992 to June 2007.

I would like to see them try and stop me [taking Holy Communion]. The cardinal's comments are unacceptable. We don't accept that Muslims should influence politics, so I don't see why Catholics should.

Adrian Piccoli, Australian NSW National Party politician, in response to Cardinal Pell commenting on political issues

I don't have a problem with church leaders or community leaders inserting themselves into this debate. I think it's perfectly reasonable, it's a really important debate. But at the same time I don't believe that there's a monopoly on morality when it comes to issues like this.

Verity Firth, Australian NSW state Labor minister, in response to Cardinal Pell commenting on political issues

Jesus was a homeless itinerant living off other people's charity. He was not a pin-up boy for the idea that God makes you rich and successful.

Marion Maddox, Australian writer of *God Under Howard*

Australia is coming of age. I know some people in Australia like to think we've got our own different culture but, in regards to religion, there's no reason why we shouldn't follow the example of the American in regards to liberty and freedom of religion.

Joseph Gutnick, Australian businessman and Jewish philanthropist

The problem with this kind of American-derived Christian discourse is that it doesn't ring true with a large percentage of the Australian population.

Carole Cusack, Australian academic

Business has got its own ethics and principles. I'd like to think that I'm using my business principles appropriately, but I don't mix it with my religious feelings.

Frank Lowy, Australian-Hungarian, co-founder of The Westfield Group

God led me to Gloria Jean's and to take this opportunity to build a business that can help the community.

Peter Irvine, Australian managing director of Gloria Jean's coffee franchises

If you don't have a belief in God, who are you accountable to? You in effect have become your own God.

Roger Corbett, Australian Reserve Bank director and former CEO of Woolworths

I often ask: how did Jesus become pro-rich, pro-war and only pro-American?

Jim Wallace, American author of *God's Politics*

Our banking system grew by accident; and whenever something happens by accident, it becomes a religion.

Walter Wriston (1919–2005), American banker and former chairman of Citicorp

Politics in America is the binding secular religion.

Theodore Harold White (1915–1986), American political journalist, historian, and novelist

The whole peninsula [Sinai] ... remains what it has always been: one of the last great wildernesses of the world, a place of stunning beauty and harsh reality where history, religion and modern politics come together as nowhere else.

Terence Smith, American journalist

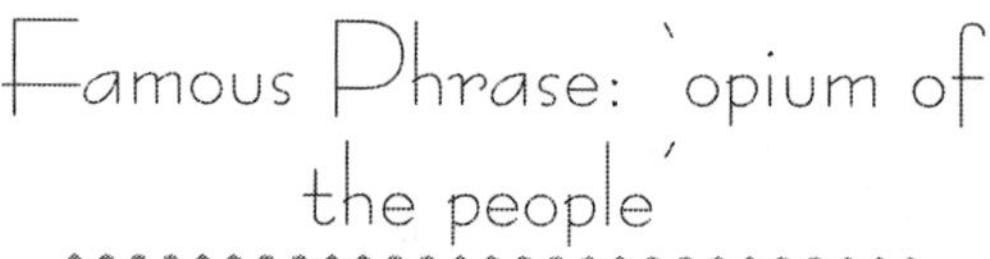

Religious suffering is, at one and the same time, the expression of real suffering and a protest against real suffering. Religion is the sigh of the oppressed creature, the heart of a heartless world, and the soul of soulless conditions. It is the opium of the people.

Karl Marx (1818–1883), British-Prussian political philosopher

Rhetoric, speechifying or spin

I have no plans to attack on my desk.

George W. Bush, American president, comment from 2002 about plans to invade Iraq

Look, our strategy is to create chaos, to create a vacuum ... We will export death and violence to the four corners of the earth in defense of our great nation.

George W. Bush

You can fool some of the people all of the time, and those are the ones you want to concentrate on.

George W. Bush

God told me to strike at al Qaeda and I struck them, and then he instructed me to strike at Saddam, which I did.

George W. Bush. The Israeli newspaper *Haaretz* took this quote from transcripts of negotiating sessions meeting between Palestinian Prime Minister Mahmoud Abbas and Bush.

I have no plans, and no plans to plan.

Mario Cuomo, American Democrat politician and former New York City mayor about plans to run for the presidency

You campaign in poetry. You govern in prose.

Mario Cuomo

We think this election is about more than 'cash for trash'.

Bill Clinton, former American president, during 1992 presidential election campaign

If you'll be my voice today, I'll be yours for the next four years.

Bill Clinton, when he had laryngitis during the last days of the 1992 presidential election campaign

I experimented with marijuana a time or two. And I didn't like it, and I didn't inhale.

Bill Clinton, former American president during 1992 presidential campaign

Early to bed, early to rise, work like hell and advertise.

Ted Turner, American businessman and founder of CNN

As long as you're going to be thinking anyway, think big.

Donald Trump, American businessman

Let's make a dent in the universe.

Steve Jobs, American businessman and founder of Apple Computers about his ambitions for his company

This administration today, here and now, declares unconditional war on poverty in America.

Lyndon Baines Johnson (1908–1973), American president

We will decide who comes here and the circumstances in which they come.

John Howard, Australian Prime Minister about the controversy following the Australian government's refusal to accept refugees rescued in Australian waters by a Norwegian merchant ship

With the casino and the beds, our passengers will have at least two ways to get lucky on one of our flights.

Sir Richard Branson, British businessman and founder of the Virgin Group

'Impossible' n'est pas français.

Napoleon I (1769–1821), French military leader and emperor

The bullet that will kill me is not yet cast.

Napoleon I

You've got to sing like you don't need the money.

Glenda Jackson, British Labour politician and former actor

Since becoming a central banker, I have learned to mumble with great incoherence. If I seem unduly clear to you, you must have misunderstood what I said.

Alan Greenspan, American economist and former chairman of the board of governors of the Federal Reserve

They'll be the spin doctors, senior advisers to the candidates, and they'll be playing for very high stakes. How well they do their work could be as important as how well the candidates do theirs.

Jack Rosenthal, in a *New York Times* editorial, after a Reagan-Mondale presidential debate

We should put the spin doctors in spin clinics, where they can meet other spin patients and be treated by spin consultants. The rest of us can get on with the proper democratic process.

Tony Benn, former British Labour minister

Leaking is what you do; briefing is what I do.

James Callaghan (1912–2005), British Labor prime minister

He steps on stage and draws the sword of rhetoric, and when he is through, someone is lying wounded and thousands of others are either angry or consoled.

Pete Hamill, American journalist, novelist, and short story writer, about New York City Mayor Edward Koch

Famous Phrase: 'axis of evil'

States like these ... constitute an axis of evil, arming to threaten the peace of this world.

George W. Bush, American president in his 2002 State of the Union speech characterising his administration's attitude to the rogue states Iran, Iraq and North Korea

Success

Success is that old ABC—ability, breaks and courage.

Charles Luckman (1909–1999), American architect and businessman

Success is a lousy teacher. It seduces smart people into thinking they can't lose.

Bill Gates, American, Microsoft co-founder and *Forbes* richest man in the world since 1995

Bill Gates is a very rich man today … and do you want to know why? The answer is one word: versions.

Dave Barry, American comedian

In a knowledge society, we expect everyone to be a success. This is clearly an impossibility. For a great many people, there is at best an absence of failure.

Peter Drucker (1909–2005), American-Austrian management academic and writer

Canada was supposed to be British government, French culture, and American know-how. Instead it got French government, American culture and British know-how.

Lester Pearson (1897–1972), Canadian Liberal prime minister

If 'A' is a success in life, then A = x + y + z. Work is x; y is play, and z is keeping your mouth shut.

Albert Einstein (1879–1955), American-German physicist

Those who have succeeded at anything and don't mention luck are kidding themselves.

Larry King, American broadcaster

The secret of our success is people. If you can find the right people, look after those people, you can achieve pretty well anything.

Sir Richard Branson, British businessman and founder of the Virgin Group

Any doctor can bury his mistakes but an architect can only advise his client to plant vines.

Frank Lloyd Wright (1867–1959), American architect

Think of yourself as on the threshold of unparalleled success. A whole clear, glorious life lies before you. Achieve! Achieve!

Andrew Carnegie (1835–1919), American-Scottish businessman

In the scientific community it's publish or perish, whereas in the commercial arena it's publish and perish.

Marie Stoner, Australian businesswoman and co-founder of Clinical Cell Culture about the difference between the business world and academia

Confidence is the expectation of success. When you expect success, you are willing to put in the effort to achieve it.

Rosabeth Moss Kanter, American management academic

Famous Phrase: 'the greasy pole'

I have climbed to the top of the greasy pole.

Benjamin Disraeli (1804–1881), British prime minister

Taxes are the price we pay for a civilised society.

Oliver Wendell Holmes Jr (1841–1935), American Supreme Court judge

Taxes are not good things, but if you want services, somebody's got to pay for them so they're a necessary evil.

Michael Bloomberg, American businessman and New York City mayor

Taxes are the sinews of the state.

Marcus Tullius Cicero (106 BC–46 AD), Roman statesman and philosopher

We don't pay taxes. Only the little people pay taxes.

Leona Helmsley (1920–2007), American businesswoman jailed for tax evasion

I told the Inland Revenue I didn't owe them a penny because I lived near the seaside.

Ken Dodd, English comedian

I am in favour of cutting taxes under any circumstances and for any excuse, for any reason, whenever it's possible.

Milton Friedman (1912–2006), American economist

Inflation is the one form of taxation that can be imposed without legislation.

Milton Friedman

Let them march all they want, as long as they continue to pay their taxes.

Alexander Haig, American general and chief of staff to Ronald Reagan

The avoidance of taxes is the only intellectual pursuit that still carries any reward.

John Maynard Keynes (1883–1946), British economist

The rich aren't like us, they pay less taxes.

Peter de Vries (1910–93), American writer

The way to crush the bourgeoisie is to grind them between the millstones of taxation and inflation.

Vladimir Lenin (1870–1925), Russian revolutionary and first leader of the Soviet Union

I'm proud to pay taxes. I pay a lot of taxes, but it sure beats the alternative.

Payne Stewart (1957–1999), American golfer

Famous Phrase: 'death and taxes'

In this world nothing can be said to be certain, except death and taxes.

Benjamin Franklin (1706–1790), American politician and 'founding father'

Technology

The first rule of any technology used in a business is that automation applied to an efficient operation will magnify the efficiency. The second is that automation applied to an inefficient operation will magnify the inefficiency.

Bill Gates, American, Microsoft co-founder and *Forbes* richest man in the world since 1995

Spam will be a thing of the past in two years' time.

Bill Gates in 2004

The Internet is the most important development in mass communications since the invention of the printing press.

Bill Gates in 1997

We live in a society exquisitely dependent on science and technology, in which hardly anyone knows anything about science and technology.

Carl Sagan (1934–1996), American astronomist

Bill Gates is the pope of the personal computer industry. He decides who's going to build.

Larry Ellison, American business executive and co-founder of Oracle Corporation

War is too serious a business to be left to computers.

Art Buchwald (1925–2007), American newspaper columnist

There is always a lot of Utopianism around any new piece of technology. I think when television was invented people talked a lot about how it would promote universal peace. But what do we have? A lot of sitcoms and game shows.

Marc Andreessen, American software engineer and businessman

What's my return on investment in e-commerce? Are you crazy? This is Columbus in the New World. What was his ROI?

Andrew Grove, American–Hungarian business executive and co-founder of Intel

When the printing press was invented, people said, 'What's the use of printing when only a few people can read?' People in virtually all societies will, by the first decade of the 21st century, be able to communicate through these broadband digital networks and information highways.

Arthur C. Clarke, English science fiction writer

You have zero privacy. Get over it.

Scott McNealy, American, co-founder and former Sun Microsystems CEO

The only thing that I'd rather own than Windows is English, because then I could charge you $249 for the right to speak it.

Scott McNealy

I don't want my kids growing up in a world of 'control–alt–delete'.

Scott McNealy

Too much talk focuses on the technology, even worse on the speed of the gadget, always faster, faster.

Peter Drucker (1909–2005), American-Austrian management academic and writer

Can we really expect millions of busy people to get in their car, drive to a store, pick out a movie, stand in line, fill out a rental agreement, pay a deposit, drive home, play it on their VCR and then, the next day, repeat the procedure in reverse to return it?

Steven Ross (1927–1992), American businessman

If we had similar progress in automotive technology, today you could buy a Lexus for about $2. It would travel at the speed of sound and go about 600 miles on a thimble of gas.

Randall Tobias, American businessman, AT&T chairman

You go to your TV set when you want to turn your brain off. You go to your computer when you want to turn your brain on.

Steve Jobs, American businessman and founder of Apple Computers

Bill Gates is not necessarily so different from the rest of us. I went into his den and his VCR is still flashing 12:00.

Jay Leno, American TV talkshow host and comedian

One in which every adult American was educated well enough to be able to programme the clock timer on his video recorder.

George Bush Sr, former American president, about how he would like his presidency remembered

In politics I think it is wiser to leave five minutes too soon than to continue for five years too long.

John Biffen (1930–2007), British Conservative politician in his resignation letter

There is more to life than increasing its speed.

Mahatma Gandhi (1869–1948), Indian independence movement leader and pacifist

There are two kinds of chancellor. Those who fail and those who get out in time.

Gordon Brown, British Labour prime minister, comment from 2005 when he was Chancellor of the Exchequer

Sometimes, when they say you're ahead of your time, it's just a polite way of saying you have a real bad sense of timing.

George McGovern, American Democrat politician

The government, in due course, acted promptly.

Geoffrey O'Halloran Giles (1923–90), Australian Liberal politician

By the year 2000 I would like to see an Australian nation that feels comfortable and relaxed about three things: I would like to see them comfortable and relaxed about their history; I would like to see them comfortable and relaxed about the present, and I'd also like to see them comfortable and relaxed about the future.

John Howard, Australian Prime Minister during the 1996 federal election campaign

It is best not to swap horses when crossing streams.

Abraham Lincoln (1809–1865), American president

Trust me

Without trust you cannot get extraordinary things done. Exemplary leaders are devoted to creating a climate of trust based on mutual respect and caring.

James Kouzes and Barry Posner, American management writers

I will tell you what leadership is. It's Jack Kennedy refusing to risk nuclear war when nearly everyone in the room is telling him to.

Robert McNamara, former American secretary of defence, comment in his 80s about the Cuban missile crisis during the early 1960s

My experience of gentlemen's agreements is that, when it comes to the pinch, there are rarely enough bloody gentlemen about.

Ben Chifley (1885–1951), Australian Labor prime minister

It is always the best policy to speak the truth—unless, of course, you are an exceptionally good liar.

Jerome K. Jerome (1859–1927), British writer

An honest politician is one who when he is bought stays bought.

Simon Cameron (1799–1889), American secretary of War during Abraham Lincoln's presidency

She tells enough white lies to ice a wedding cake.

Margot Asquith (1864–1945), British socialite and wife of prime minister Herbert Asquith

The road to tyranny, we must never forget, begins with the destruction of the truth.

Bill Clinton, former American president

Telling the whole truth is an impossible standard.

Douglas J. Feith, former American Undersecretary of Defense and advocate for invasion of Iraq in 2003

Since a politician never believes what he says, he's quite surprised to be taken at his word.

Charles de Gaulle (1890–1970), French president

The [Supreme] Court's only armor is the cloak of public trust; its sole ammunition, the collective hopes of our society.

Irving R. Kaufman (1910–1992), American federal judge

Let's talk sense to the American people. Let's tell them the truth, that there are no gains with pains.

Adlai Stevenson (1900–1965), American Democrat politician during a presidential election campaign

If they will stop telling lies about the Democrats, we will stop telling the truth about them.

Adlai Stevenson about his Republican opponents

Behind every great fortune there is a crime.

Honore de Balzac (1799–1850), French novelist

A lie can travel halfway around the world while the truth is putting on its shoes.

Mark Twain (1835–1910), American writer

If you tell the truth you don't have to remember anything.

Mark Twain (1835–1910), American writer

News is a business, but it is also a public trust.

Dan Rather, American news anchor

The only way to make a man trustworthy is to trust him.

Henry Lewis Stimson (1867–1950), American statesman

Never trust the judgment of an enthusiastic man; never trust the promises of a lazy one.

Mason Cooley (1927–2002), American aphorist

Trust, but look for the exits.

Mason Cooley

Famous Phrase: 'keep the bastards honest'

The Australian Democrats will keep the bastards honest if they win the balance of power at the Senate election.

Don Chipp (1925–2006), Australian politician and founder of the Australian Democrats

Vision

We have a great objective—the light on the hill—which we aim to reach by working for the betterment of mankind not only here but anywhere we may give a helping hand.

Ben Chifley (1885–1951), Australian prime minister

Capital isn't scarce; vision is.

Sam Walton (1918–1992), American, Wal-Mart founder

In order to serve its purpose, a vision has to be a shared vision.

Warren Bennis, American management writer and consultant

If you are clear about your vision and honest about your present realities, you don't have to figure everything out. Things start happening of their own accord.

Ken Blanchard and Jesse Stoner, American management consultants and writers

If you think Daddy had trouble with 'the vision thing', wait till you meet this one.

Molly Ivins and Lou Dubose, American journalists in their 2000 book *Shrub* about George Bush Sr and George Bush Jr

Emotions you can wear on your sleeve in the short term but long term you have to be very much focused on your vision.

Paul Little, Australian business executive and managing director of Toll Holdings

If we like a man's dream, we call him a reformer; if we don't like his dream, we call him a crank.

William Dean Howells (1837–1920), American writer

I'm not a great visionary. My main message to the kids is do what lights your fire. It's better to be passionate about what you do than just grind it out like a lawyer or something.

Scott McNealy, American, co-founder and former Sun Microsystems CEO

If I'd asked the public about their transport needs, they would have told me to invent a faster horse.

Henry Ford (1863–1947), American, founder of the Ford Motor Company

A dream is just a dream. A goal is a dream with a plan and a deadline.

Harvey Mackay, American, founder and CEO of the Mackay Envelope Company

A vision of things that has no room for the inner life is bankrupt, but a psychology without social analysis or politics is both powerless and very lonely.

Joseph Featherstone, American social critic

Europe is in danger of plunging into world peace.

Boris Yeltsin (1931–2007), Russian president

No wars are unintended or 'accidental'. What is often unintended is the length and bloodiness of the war. Defeat too is unintended.

Geoffrey Blainey, Australian historian and writer

If you want to make peace with your enemy, you have to work with your enemy. Then he becomes your partner.

Nelson Mandela, former South African president

When the rich wage war it's the poor who die.

Jean-Paul Sartre (1905–1980), French philosopher and writer

Weapons are like money; no-one knows the meaning of enough.

Martin Amis, British novelist

I've been to war, and it's not easy to kill. It's bloody and messy and totally horrifying, and the consequences are serious.

Oliver Stone, American film director

Peace is much more precious than a piece of land.

Anwar al–Sadat (1918–1981), Egyptian president

It is far easier to make war than to make peace.

Georges Clemenceau (1841–1929), French statesman

Revolution is the festival of the oppressed.

Germaine Greer, Australian feminist, writer and academic

Wars are not paid for in wartime, the bill comes later.

Benjamin Franklin (1706–1790), American politician and 'founding father'

Non-violence is the first article of my faith. It is also the last article of my creed.

Mahatma Gandhi (1869–1948), Indian independence movement leader and pacifist

The moment the slave resolves that he will no longer be a slave, his fetters fall. He frees himself and shows the way to others. Freedom and slavery are mental states.

Mahatma Gandhi

I know not with what weapons World War III will be fought, but World War IV will be fought with sticks and stones.

Albert Einstein (1879–1955), American-German physicist

They found more dangerous chemicals in Coca-Cola's Dasani mineral water than they did in the whole of Iraq.

Robin Cook (1946–2005), British Labour politician, following the 2003 invasion of Iraq based on the threat of Saddam's 'weapons of mass destruction'

Older men declare war. But it is youth who must fight and die.

Herbert Hoover (1874–1964), American president

If it was not for the presence of foreign troops on Australian soil during World War II, people like Mr Gould be pulling rickshaws up George Street.

George Shortell, an ALP 2007 conference delegate, about a protestor

Politics and war are remarkably similar situations.

Newt Gingrich, American Republican politician

We make war that we may live in peace.

Aristotle (384–322BC), Greek philosopher

The Falklands thing was fought between two bald men over a comb.

Jorge Luis Borges (1899–1986), Argentinean writer (based on an Argentinean proverb)

There never was a good war, or a bad peace.

Benjamin Franklin (1706–1790), American politician and 'founding father'

It is not possible to create peace in the Middle East by jeopardising the peace of the world.

Aneurin Bevan (1897–1960), British politician abut the Suez crisis

Six days of war followed by 40 years of misery.

Headline from *The Economist*, 26 May 2007, about the 1967 Six Days War

The Gulf War was like teenage sex. We got in too soon and out too soon.

Tom Harkin, American Democrat senator about the 1991 Gulf War

We've got the kind of president who thinks arms control means some kind of deodorant.

Patricia Schroeder, American Democrat politician about President Ronald Reagan

This will be a campaign unlike any other in history. A campaign characterised by shock, by surprise, by flexibility, by the employment of precise munitions on a scale never before seen, and by the application of overwhelming force.

Tommy Franks, American army general who led the military invasion into Iraq in 2003

Wars are popular. Contractors make profits; the aristocracy glean honour.

Ramsay MacDonald (1866–1937), British Labour prime minister

Politics is war without bloodshed while war is politics with bloodshed.

Mao Zedong (1893–1976), first leader of Communist China

Famous Phrase: 'peace for our time'

This is the second time in our history that there has come back from Germany to Downing Street peace with honour. I believe it is peace for our time.

Neville Chamberlain (1869–1940), British prime minister, said on 30 September 1938, less than a year before the declaration of WWII

War on terror

It is time for us to win the first war of the 21st century.

George W. Bush, on 16 September 2001 in a speech to the American Congress five days after the terrorist attacks in New York and Washington

This crusade, this war on terrorism, is going to take a little while.

George W. Bush, press conference 16 September 2001

In the fight against terrorism, the United States welcomed Australian military participation ...

John Howard, Australian Prime Minister 25 October 2001

If I were running al-Qaeda in Iraq, I would put a circle around March 2008, and be praying as many times as possible for a victory not only for Obama, but also for the Democrats.

John Howard, about Barack Obama's plans to withdraw American troops from Iraq if he won the American presidency in 2008

I think it's flattering that one of George Bush's allies on the other side of the world started attacking me the day after I announced my candidature. I would also note that we have close to 140,000 troops in Iraq, and my understanding is that Mr Howard has deployed 1400, so if he is to fight the good fight in Iraq, I would suggest that he calls up another 20,000 Australians and sends them to Iraq.

Barack Obama, American Democrat presidential candidate

The time for us to ask how to get out of Iraq was before we got in.

Barack Obama

Terrorism is the war of the poor, and war is the terrorism of the rich.

Peter Ustinov (1921–2004), British actor

The research suggests that you are more likely to be killed by a vending machine than you are by a terrorist, here at home.

David Wright-Neville, Australian counter-terrorism researcher

Terrorism is the tactic of demanding the impossible, and demanding it at gunpoint.

Christopher Hitchens, British-American writer

Who needs al-Qaeda when you have *E. coli*?

Jay Inslee, American Democrat politician, about a 2007 scandal that involved tainted imported food into America

Democratic nations must try to find ways to starve the terrorist and the hijacker of the oxygen of publicity on which they depend.

Margaret Thatcher, former British prime minister

Warren Buffett

Warren Buffett is an American investor, businessperson and philanthropist. As a legendary share market investor Buffett, aka 'Oracle of Omaha', is often quoted and his words encapsulate his investment philosophy simply but memorably.

Price is what you pay. Value is what you get.

Most people get interested in stocks when everyone else is. The time to get interested is when no one else is. You can't buy what is popular and do well.

I'd be a bum on the street with a tin cup if the markets were always efficient.

The most important quality for an investor is temperament, not intellect ... You need a temperament that neither derives great pleasure from being with the crowd or against the crowd.

The business schools reward difficult complex behaviour more than simple behaviour, but simple behaviour is more effective.

It's only when the tide goes out that you learn who's been swimming naked.

Wide diversification is only required when investors do not understand what they are doing.

Only buy something that you'd be perfectly happy to hold if the market shut down for 10 years.

We simply attempt to be fearful when others are greedy and to be greedy only when others are fearful.

Why not invest your assets in the companies you really like? As Mae West said, too much of a good thing can be wonderful.

Our favourite holding period is forever.

A public opinion poll is no substitute for thought.

We enjoy the process far more than the proceeds.

It takes 20 years to build a reputation and five minutes to ruin it. If you think about that, you'll do things differently.

A very rich person should leave his kids enough to do anything but not enough to do nothing.

The smarter the journalists are, the better off society is. [For] to a degree, people read the press to inform themselves—and the better the teacher, the better the student body.

Someone's sitting in the shade today because someone planted a tree a long time ago.

Managers thinking about accounting issues should never forget one of Abraham Lincoln's favourite riddles: 'How many legs does a dog have if you call his tail a leg?' The answer: 'Four, because calling a tail a leg does not make it a leg'.

Wealth, wisdom and happiness

Life is a game. Money is how we keep score.

Ted Turner, American businessman and founder of CNN

If you can actually count your money, you are not really a rich man.

J. Paul Getty (1892–1976), American oil billionaire and art collector

Anybody who thinks money will make you happy, hasn't got money.

David Geffen, American record executive and businessman

After a certain point, money is meaningless. It ceases to be the goal. The game is what counts.

Aristotle Onassis (1906–1975), Greek billionaire

Except for the occasional heart attack, I never felt better.

Dick Cheney, American vice president

What's the quickest way to become a millionaire? Borrow fivers off everyone you meet.

Sir Richard Branson, British businessman and founder of the Virgin Group

There is no doubt if you mix in the right circles, vis a vis making money, not having fun, you will learn a hell of a lot. In the 1980s, I made sure I mixed with Kerry Packer.

Rene Rivkin (1944–2005), Australian businessman

I used to believe that anything was better than nothing. Now I know that sometimes nothing is better.

Glenda Jackson, British Labour politician and former actor

Sydney epitomises the new dispensation, a city now divided by the haves and the have-yachts.

Sally Warhaft, Australian editor of *The Monthly*

Once wealth and beauty are gone, there is always rural life.

Mason Cooley (1927–2002), American aphorist

All you can be sure about in a political-minded writer is that if his work should last you will have to skip the politics when you read it. Many of the so-called politically enlisted writers change their politics frequently ... Perhaps it can be respected as a form of the pursuit of happiness.

Ernest Hemingway (1899–1961), American writer

Winston Churchill

Winston Churchill (1874–1965) was the prime minister of the United Kingdom from 1940 to 1945 and 1951 to 1955. Churchill was a successful statesman, orator and strategist.

Success is never final.

I cannot forecast to you the action of Russia. It is a riddle wrapped in a mystery inside an enigma.

I have nothing to offer but blood, toil, tears, and sweat.

You ask, what is our aim? I can answer in one word: It is victory, victory at all costs, victory in spite of all terror, victory, however long and hard the road may be; for without victory, there is no survival.

Never in the field of human conflict was so much owed by so many to so few.

House of Commons speech about the Battle of Britain in 1940

We will not say thereafter that the Greeks fight like heroes, but heroes fight like the Greeks!

Now this is not the end. It is not even the beginning of the end. But it is, perhaps, the end of the beginning.

To jaw–jaw is always better than to war–war.

Anyone can rat, but it takes a certain amount of ingenuity to re-rat.

Some regard private enterprise as if it were a predatory tiger to be shot. Others look upon it as a cow that they can milk. Only a handful see it for what it really is—the strong horse that pulls the whole cart.

The inherent vice of capitalism is the unequal sharing of blessings, the inherent vice of Socialism is the equal sharing of miseries.

We shall defend our island, whatever the cost may be. We shall fight on the beaches, we shall fight on the landing–grounds, we shall fight in the fields and in the streets, we shall fight in the hills. We shall never surrender!

I am a child of the House of Commons. I was brought up in my father's house to believe in democracy.

This is the lesson: never give in, never give in, never, never, never, never—in nothing, great or small, large or petty—never give in except to convictions of honour and good sense. Never yield to force; never yield to the apparently overwhelming might of the enemy.

This report, by its very length, defends itself against the risk of being read, Sir.

Many forms of Government have been tried, and will be tried in this world of sin and woe. No one pretends that democracy is perfect or all–wise. Indeed, it has been said that democracy is the worst form of government except all those other forms that have been tried from time to time.

I do not agree that the dog in a manger has the final right to the manger even though he may have lain there for a very long time. I do not admit that right. I do not admit for instance, that a great wrong has been done to the Red Indians of America or the black people of Australia. I do not admit that a wrong has been done to these people by the fact that a stronger race, a higher-grade race, a more worldly wise race to put it that way, has come in and taken their place.

The nation had the lion's heart. I had the luck to give the road.

The art of making deep sounds from the stomach sound like important messages from the brain.

Call that a maiden speech? I call it a brazen hussy of a speech.

From Stettin in the Baltic to Trieste in the Adriatic an iron curtain has descended across the Continent.

Previously used by others from 1920 but Churchill's use of this phrase in a 1946 speech is the most famous early use of it

Women are not a niche

We are not a 'niche'.

Marti Barletta, American author of *Marketing to Women* and *Prime Time Women*

I married beneath me. All women do.

Nancy Astor (1879–1964), British-American politician

We are in the post-feminist stage of the debate. The good thing about this stage is that I think we have broken through some of the old stereotypes.

John Howard, Australian prime minister, comment from 2002

It must be nice to be on Planet Howard where all the feminist battles have been won and women get the jobs they are qualified for and the promotions they deserve.

Anne Summers, Australian writer and feminist

I know I have but the body of a weak and feeble woman; but I have the heart of a king, and of a king of England too ...

Queen Elizabeth I (1533–1633), British monarch, to her military forces prior to a battle against Spain

Women sometimes bend the wrong way just to prove themselves to men, but when we learn to listen to ourselves, that will be revolutionary.

Jane Fonda, American actor and intermittent activist

The worker is the slave of capitalist society, the female worker is the slave of that slave.

James Connolly (1868–1916), Irish socialist politician

Feminism is the most revolutionary idea there has ever been. Equality for women demands a change in the human psyche more profound than anything Marx dreamed of. It means valuing parenthood as much as we value banking.

Polly Toynbee, British journalist

Somewhere out in this audience may even be someone who will one day follow in my footsteps, and preside over the White House as the President's spouse. I wish him well!

Barbara Bush, former American First Lady

Today the problem that has no name is how to juggle work, love, home and children.

Betty Friedan (1921–2006), American feminist and writer

I long for the day when a new generation of Anita Roddicks can address the AGM in a bright pink dress and strappy sandals.

Alexandra Shulman, British journalist

Why join a women's group to lobby government ministers when you can become a minister yourself?

Pauline Toner (1935–1989), first Victorian female minister appointed to state government in 1982

You can have it all but not all at the same time.

Quentin Bryce, Australian feminist and Queensland governor

It was a big step up for a lady, and she did it very well and she should be recognised for that. It shouldn't be clouded by one tempestuous, unpredictable juggernaut of an event like that takeover bid.

James Strong, Australian business executive about Qantas chairwoman, Margaret Jackson

If you want something said, ask a man. If you want something done, ask a woman.

Margaret Thatcher, former British prime minister

She is clearly the best man among them.

Barbara Castle (1910–2002), British Labour politician, about Margaret Thatcher

Clearly, society has a tremendous stake in insisting on a woman's natural fitness for the career of mother: the alternatives are all too expensive.

Ann Oakley, British sociologist and writer

A woman is like a tea bag—you can't tell how strong she is until you put her in hot water.

Nancy Reagan, wife of Ronald Reagan, former American president

Because I am a woman, I must make unusual efforts to succeed. If I fail, no one will say, 'She doesn't have what it takes.' They will say, 'Women don't have what it takes.'

Clare Boothe Luce (1903–1987), American writer and politician

A geisha's *raison d'être* is to pour drinks, giggle behind her hand, tell men they are handsome, strong and amusing, listen to boastful lies, and never show any emotion except bliss. Occasionally, for a great deal of cash, some will allow men to copulate with them. We, of course, have geishas back in Blighty: we call them barmaids.

A.A. Gill, British newspaper columnist

In societies where men are truly confident of their own worth, women are not merely tolerated but valued.

Aung San Suu Kyi, Burmese politician who won the 1990 democratic election but was arrested following a military coup and has been under house arrest since. This is a comment from a speech in 1995.

I could have stayed home and baked cookies and had teas. But what I decided was to fulfil my profession, which I entered before my husband was in public life.

Hillary Clinton, American Democrat politician and wife of Bill Clinton

Toughness doesn't have to come in a pinstripe suit.

Dianne Feinstein, American Democrat politician

I myself have never been able to find out precisely what feminism is; I only know that people call me a feminist whenever I express sentiments that differentiate me from a doormat or a prostitute.

Rebecca West (1892–1983), Irish writer

Index